WORK ZONE
MADNESS!

SURVIVING AND RISING ABOVE
WORKPLACE DYSFUNCTION

NANCY SLOMOWITZ

N3 Publications, LLC
Darnestown, MD

To the Reader: Names, identifying details and circumstances of the people portrayed in this book have been changed.

Published by
N3 Publications, LLC
Darnestown, Maryland

Publisher's Cataloging-in-Publication Data
Slomowitz, Nancy.
Work zone madness! : surviving and rising above workplace dysfunction / Nancy Slomowitz.—Darnestown, MD : N3 Publications, LLC, 2012.

p. ; cm.
ISBN13: 978-0-9848408-3-0 (Hard Cover)
ISBN13: 978-0-9848408-0-9 (Kindle)
ISBN13: 978-0-9848408-1-6 (ePub)
ISBN13: 978-0-9848408-2-3 (Nook)

1. Organizational effectiveness. 2. Communication in management. 3. Business ethics. 4. Work environment—Psychological aspects. 5. Slomowitz, Nancy—Anecdotes. I. Title.

HD58.9.S56 2012
658.4—dc22   2011944496

Project coordination by Jenkins Group, Inc.
www.BookPublishing.com

Cover design by Chris Rhoads
Interior design by Debbie Sidman
Interior Illustrations: Jada Fitch/thejulygroup.com

Printed in the United States of America
16 15 14 13 12 • 5 4 3 2 1

To my mother and father—
who taught me that doing the right thing is its own reward.

Contents

Foreword

Is integrity, driven by pragmatic common sense in business, a relic of the past? Of course not, but it is drowned out by the chorus of unmitigated greed and corruption that captures the headlines. The author will have none of that. In her own business, Nancy Slomowitz hires the best, compensates them well, and relies on their professionalism to enhance her product. She brings those same tenets of success to the clients she consults. And now, in her first book, she offers that same toolbox of pragmatic, commonsense tools, for a healthier workplace. It all begins with integrity, in search for the common good. It shouldn't be a novel idea.

Nancy asked that I produce a film about her company's culture of putting people before profits—and, specifically, the importance of offering a variety of traditional and nontraditional benefits to her employees. A journalistic skeptic by nature, I was struck that in this era of corporate scale-backs of all benefits, there was an employer seeking to enlighten her organization about alternative methods toward a healthier life and work environment. This was clearly counterintuitive.

During the production of the film, she encouraged my journalistic discovery, never attempting to shape it. And what I discovered was a work environment that transcended a perceived norm. Employees shared stories of encouragement for innovation, independent thinking, appreciation for and rewarding of effort, and complete support, financial and otherwise, for personal development, whatever forms it may take.

This was simply common sense. For a group dedicated to improving the efficiency of others, it makes little sense to be dysfunctional within. And I discovered her methods to be just that, common sense. Hire the best people you can, treat them well, encourage their growth, and pull it all together by offering and demanding uncompromising integrity. But if it were only so simple. . . . Obviously, it is not.

That's where *Work Zone Madness* comes in, a toolbox of pragmatic, commonsense instruments to improve the workplace, for both employer and employee. It is a beacon of light shining through the haze of greed and corruption, a primer for happiness and success through common sense and integrity.

—Jim Forbes, journalist, correspondent, and producer,
The American Entrepreneur

Introduction

What happened to being ethical, doing the right thing, and caring about more than the bottom line? Wherever we go, the news is filled with stories of greed, fraud, and other financial scandals. Closer to home, it's nearly impossible not to notice disgruntled workers and managers at our places of work, with loads of finger-pointing on both sides.

These are tough economic times, and it is easy to place blame on others or to play the victim, but to survive, we must learn how to navigate through the workplace land mines and rise above the situation. This book sheds light, in an anecdotal format, on the types of financial and human behaviors that are counterproductive to doing good business and on the myriad impediments to personal success in the workplace. I've written this book to bring these issues into the light of day so that you can recognize what is happening in your own workplace and, hopefully, take some steps to stop it.

I've spent more than thirty years working in the back office as a business advisor to private and public organizations of all types, each desperate for help in solving its structural problems and rooting out chaos. I have seen it all. I'll present examples of counterproductive behaviors, some of which you will recognize from your own workplace. I'll also provide recommendations based on my own experience for mitigating the effects of these dysfunctional behaviors. It's my hope that when you have finished this book, you will be able to identify the causes of chaos in your own company or work environment—and even if you can't eliminate them, at least you will be able to rise above them so that you can regain your sense of dignity and integrity. If enough of us do this, we will be able to bring about change that will eliminate the causes of dysfunction.

It is no exaggeration that a majority of workers and employers in the workplace today are dissatisfied. Workers feel that they are not being treated fairly, and employers feel that the employees just don't care. Unfortunately, they are both right. This book offers insights into both perspectives. This is not a business "how-to" book. This is a book about surviving in the workplace today—with perspectives and simple concepts to improve your quality of life in the workplace. As a company owner who has seen these behaviors firsthand, I can empathize with both employee and employer trying to survive in today's challenging economy. Whether you are an unhappy employee, unemployed, trying to survive a layoff, or an employer trying to stay afloat, this book offers clear and practical ways to improve your situation.

PART I

Recognizing the Dysfunction

CHAPTER 1

Inside the Glass Edifice

The new corporate headquarters was breathtakingly beautiful viewed from across the boulevard, its grand glass and marble edifice towering over a recently redeveloped tract of former inner-city slum. Once visitors entered its portal, the architectural experience was no less impressive to behold. One's attention was immediately drawn toward the heavens to the bright light filling a massive central atrium spiraling upward hundreds of feet. Closer to ground level, high-tech fixtures and ultramodern furnishings leading to the reception desk and bank of elevators further embellished the impression of corporate grandeur and invincibility.

"How are you doing?" one employee asked a colleague, breaking the silence on the elevator. "I'm here" was the sarcastic answer as the doors opened to the fourth floor. They gave each other an understated nod of recognition before going in opposite directions down the hall.

Both went to their desks and before turning on their desktop computers slipped on small earphones that had become part of the survival kit to be able to hear themselves think in the clutter of distraction that was their workplace. For all the many thousands of cubic feet dedicated to airspace in that glorious atrium, they had to take it away from somewhere else, the joke went. "So why not the elbow room?" The employees who were doing the bulk of the work required to keep the corporate machinery running were packed together like livestock into small units aptly called "the bull pen." No matter what direction their chairs swiveled, there was another body also trying to get some work done in proximity way too close for comfort.

In the bull pen, you could forget about privacy, whether it was dealing with confidential and sensitive business information or the personal chatter about a doctor's appointment, how much someone had to drink the night before, troubles with a significant other, and so on. The music in the earphones did help tune out some of the noise, but if someone were having a problem or, worse yet, acting out, it was the perfect viral breeding ground for disruption and dysfunction. The managers at least had some relief provided from a cubicle. The higher-ups had real offices with doors that closed and insulated them, so they could enjoy the decent view of the landscape through the wall of glass.

The metaphor of the atrium and the bull pen is not solely one about misbegotten priorities but is representative of what has gone awry on a core level at a shockingly high percentage of American businesses from big to small. In the same way that the worker acquiesces to an unfulfilling job and mutes dissatisfaction with the earphones, we have grown accustomed to and accepting of "business as usual" at our jobs, situations that are often unhealthy and toxic for both the bottom line and the mind and body.

Too many businesses have been entrenched for so long in the "me-me-me" mantra of self-interest ("I want it all, I want it now, and I don't care how I get it") and the throwaway mentality that we have lost sight of other ways of being. This "me"-centric approach is concerned only with taking without regard to others or the consequences.

Over the past generation, financial growth and shareholder profits have become more important than the values that support product quality and customer/employee satisfaction. This has turned broad swaths of our economy into wasteland. These days, once vibrant and robust industries and communities are looking more like ghost towns. The nutrients of our society (core values such as integrity, compassion, and concern for others) have been depleted. This book is about restoring those core values.

CHAPTER 2

The Kid in the Candy Store

Being the bearer of bad news is never fun. In my case, I frequently have to sit down with very important people who have built highly successful enterprises and help them understand why things have gone to hell. They may be leaders with corner offices on the top floor, but I have to tell them delicately that their whole place has, in effect, become a cesspool of disorder and dysfunction. I explain to them further that they basically need to go back to remedial class to understand the finances of their businesses. Delivering this message has to be handled in a sensitive manner because I don't want them to think they are idiots—because they are not.

The fact that they are coming to me in the first place shows a lot of courage. It is a big step for a big ego to declare, "I'm in serious trouble, and I need help." And most of the people who come to me have big egos—generally one of the driving factors for their success. In most cases, they've heard about me from some referral, and they're usually desperate and close to, if not already at, rock bottom. That's a good thing because I know I'll have their undivided attention. The first step to recovery is the recognition of the problem, the same prerequisite that an alcoholic or drug addict must have if treatment has any chance of success.

This was the case with Phillip, a new client. "I can't make payroll, and my controller is telling me that we have a cash flow problem. But I can't figure out where the problem is. I understand that you can help me clean this up," he said to me at our first meeting. He was a classic example of an asleep-at-the-wheel boss, now trying to recover from a head-on collision. It goes without saying that the big reason why I was in Phillip's office was due to the fact that something had gone terribly wrong with the financial management of his company.

"Let's talk about the problem, how it can be fixed, and what needs to happen here," I replied in as gentle but firm a tone as possible. I told him that I would start by examining his company's accounting system, checkbook, and bank statements; following the inflows and outflows of the cash thread; and performing a layer-by-layer analysis of income and expenses in order to reach the root cause of his problem.

In almost every case like Phillip's, I am sitting with someone who has lost control of the situation or perhaps never had control of it from the beginning. What lies underneath it all runs the gamut from wishful thinking, ignorance, and complacency to arrogance, greed, and downright evil. It plagues small companies that started with a great idea and grew too fast and mega corporations and government agencies where problems and perpetrators can easily escape detection. What they all have in common due to this negligence are the ramifications that have now stopped them in their tracks—burdened with all the needless stress, waste, and expense. If they continue to avoid cleaning up the problem, it will grow only more complicated and increasingly destructive to their businesses.

"Your service is really great, but your infrastructure just isn't there," I explained to Phillip after I had performed my analysis. "We really need to rebuild your foundation or you're not going to be able to move forward,"

I said, breaking the news like I was a carpenter called in to install new kitchen cabinets in his home, only to hammer into crumbling walls. "In fact, unless we do so, your company is probably going to go bankrupt. You don't have a real accounting system—you've cobbled together a collection of systems that were never intended to be used for accounting. As a result, you can't run reports, there are no checks and balances, and you can't tell where you are financially—and you aren't keeping your records up to date." Phillip's problems had stayed well hidden for a while but had now imploded. This is when the real problems became clear and when things began to get really interesting. Numbers do not lie—but people do. I had uncovered the layers of his financial problems; however, I was just learning about the layers of his people problems.

Phillip was a genuinely nice man, a good case study of how nice people sometimes do deceitful things—not because they are evil but because they are human. He was the classic kid in the candy store. He wanted what he wanted and put on his blinders to the ticking-time-bomb consequences of his actions. Here was a sixty-year-old man with a demanding, spoiled, and much younger wife who he could not get to stop spending huge amounts of money. His weakness for indulging his wife's regular requests for increasingly expensive toys compounded the underlying financial problems of the company. He was blindly spending funds intended to meet current employee payroll on things such as personal bonuses, a new company car for his wife, lavish meals, expensive trips, and the list goes on. These were only some of the non-business items being attributed to business expenses that he just couldn't afford.

His controller, a single, very attractive young woman, looked up to Phillip as a father figure, and they had a good rapport. She also worked well with customers and split her time between project and financial activities. She wanted to please Phillip and, as a result, abandoned her ethics and paid all the bills while knowing full well that many were not business expenses. She knew better but didn't want to say no. A good controller would have at least established the budget and prepared monthly reports against the budget. That piece was completely missing from the financial management of the organization. Phillip's company was therefore bleeding because of three factors: his overindulgence of his wife; his overdependence on one person—his controller—who didn't tell him that he couldn't afford these expenses; and his failure to insist on a traditional accounting system with regular reports.

Rarely do I encounter an R-rated situation, but I soon found out that Phillip's predicament went far beyond mere financial problems. It was a prime example of just how easily things can go wrong and how messy things can get before the bleeding is stopped. As close as I had to work with the controller, I continued to hear her claim that she and Phillip were "just good friends"—right up to the fireworks. One day, all hell finally broke loose, and everyone ran for cover. Phillip's wife came in and confronted Phillip about his affair in full view of everyone in the office, screaming and yelling obscenities galore with nary a regard for the onlookers. Think of this as *Fatal Attraction* for financial managers who need to be scared straight.

This saga demonstrates how the conscious avoidance of financial responsibility can mushroom from an under-the-radar issue into a full-blown crisis when the business owner hands the job carte blanche to someone else, someone who may or may not have the best interests of the company at heart. Had Phillip insisted on an accounting system with regular reports, he would have been able to see why he was having cash flow problems.

Let's face it. It is natural to put off the things we least enjoy or bury them at the bottom of the stack. Accounting is not a sexy thing and it does not generate any revenue by itself. It is a hard cost of doing business. What sounds more enticing: "I worked on an exciting, revenue-generating customer project" or "I closed the books for the month"? Phillip had hired someone to manage his accounting function for him. He had hired the person because he liked her. She had the credentials, she was attractive, and she had a great personality. However, she was more interested in the social aspects of the job and working with the customers than the responsibilities of a controller and the best interests of the company.

If others see that the boss is not taking an active role in overseeing the financial affairs, they will take shortcuts and cover up their mistakes and may even divert funds for their own use. Losses through mismanagement, inefficiencies, and potentially even fraud will start to pile up but will seldom be noticed right away if an effective system of oversight is lacking. The truth will eventually come forward, uncovered perhaps by a tax preparer, an outside firm doing the year-end audit, or someone like me, but the damage will have already been done.

"You're not alone in this—it is a common thing that happens," I told Phillip and have told others in the same boat. I made it clear that I was not asking him to become a CPA but just to understand the underlying structure he needed to truly support his business. With a bit of coaching, I assured him, I could give him a bulletproof system that would put his house in order and virtually eliminate the possibility of mismanagement and fraud. That process entails creating effective checks and balances on all systems and employees, eliminating single points of failure, and implementing systematic changes that I will illustrate in greater detail later. With this system in place, he would be aware of the impact of his actions before he took them. He might still be the kid in the candy store, but his eyes would be wide open, and it would become a conscious decision.

CHAPTER 3

The Derailed Train

The best way to prevent the kinds of escalating problems Phillip experienced is to have a rock-solid foundation from day one when the doors open. In far too many cases, the grunt work to get this process off on the right track is bypassed, especially in start-ups. It is intoxicating for a business owner to see what was once just a good idea on a laptop suddenly become a profitable reality and to smile watching the dollars flow in. But a hangover is sure to follow if the owner is not prepared for the complications that naturally come once things begin to really take off. Most find out the hard way just how vulnerable they are when handling the consequences of success. Taking the time and money to set things up right from the start can make a crucial difference when things begin to heat up, but it is often a tough sell to an excited entrepreneur full of confidence about his or her creation. Entrepreneurs don't want to or can't think about infrastructure. All too often they are not structured—an overabundance of creativity with a lack of business sensibility.

Because so many company owners don't set up their infrastructures correctly, most of my work consists of diagnosing the sources of their problems and building what should have been there all along. It's difficult to build an infrastructure into an established company, much like trying to repair a locomotive while it is rushing down the tracks at full speed—not impossible but very challenging. Only rarely do I have the chance to help someone build a sound infrastructure from scratch, but my friend Ari gave me just such an opportunity.

A few years back, Ari was a hot handbag designer—on top of the world. We had met at a trunk show put on by major department store; I was invited by a saleswoman who thought I would find exactly what I was looking for there. I had in mind a particular handbag for a holiday party, but I couldn't find anything I thought was right. The saleslady said, "Come on over and I'll introduce you to our designer," who happened to be Ari. I thought it was worth going to the trunk show to see what this new designer had to offer. I went to the show with a determined "just find the damned bag" attitude. But what I saw immediately excited me. "Wow, this is really cool!" I thought. Ari had this funny, larger-than-life personality, and I could see that he had enormous talent. Long story short, I ended up not only with one of his bags but also with something much better—getting to know Ari as a person and becoming his friend.

Of course, I wasn't the only person who loved Ari's stuff. A huge list of celebrities also drooled over his innovative creations and used his cell phone number like a hotline whenever they needed something special in a flash. One of Ari's handbags became the necessary accessory for runway parties and other glamorous events. Open up fashion magazines such as *Vogue* and you would often see something by Ari. The money flowed in fast and easy.

I found the perfect bag to complement my dress and returned to the trunk show to say good-bye to Ari. Before we parted, we made plans to meet up soon on my next trip to New York City. A few weeks later, I toured his showroom and we had lunch, a habit we've continued through the months and years that have followed. We became fast friends.

As time went by, I also got to know Ari's partner, Julian. Their relationship was unsteady, and that began to take its toll on the business. At a certain point, it was clear that the personal relationship was deteriorating. The business part continued but became more and more awkward as the personal relationship died. I could see the train wreck coming, and it did.

My father often repeated to me his secret to creating a sound business. It boiled down to two things: "low overhead" and "no partners." This simple yet profound advice has been at the core of my own business success. If only I had met Ari several years earlier, I could have imparted my father's wisdom to him and prevented this sad situation.

What made matters more difficult for Ari was that he had entrusted his partner with all of the business dealings. On the positive side, it had turned Ari loose as the creative half of the partnership to do his thing. But when the partnership ended, Ari was left with only half of the capabilities necessary to manage a successful business—the creative side. Completely devastated as both his personal relationship and his business dreams were dying, Ari left the country for Milan and relocated to an area near one of the factories that had manufactured his handbags. This was far enough away from the emotional devastation of his situation, he reckoned. For a year, he took a sabbatical, mourned the death of his dream and his partnership, and lived off of his savings until he was ready to reengage.

In Milan, Ari had a new idea. He had always been an animal-lover and thought he could make really elegant bags without using leather. Inspired by this new idea, he began once again to put his passion into his work. From the photos he sent me, I thought his new creations were even more remarkable and distinctive than the old, and I encouraged him to continue. From afar, he made a deal with a contact he knew in New York to operate a showroom and market his new line in the city. Things were moving forward and looking up once again for Ari. But there was one big problem—he was still not engaged in managing the business side of his new venture.

I grew worried and sent him an e-mail when I hadn't heard from him for a while. He wrote back, "You've reached out to me at one of the lowest points of my life. I know I need your help." Then I heard his story.

"I finished my samples, and I relied on this person in New York to do my showroom," he explained. But when repeated requests for a status report went unanswered, Ari suspected something was terribly wrong and flew in from Milan to the horror of discovering that his showroom was a big mirage. Everything along with it, including the last pennies he had spent creating his line, had evaporated into thin air.

"First, I need you to be my customer," Ari implored. I told him that was a given and arranged to purchase a number of items from his new collection. The next steps were to stabilize him and help him regain his confidence. Then, I explained to him what he needed to do from a business perspective. We worked out a concept for a business plan and arranged for an infusion of capital so that he could continue to get his new collection ready for market. We started communicating regularly so we could adjust his plans as events unfolded, and we continue to do so.

Ari made several critical mistakes. The first was not taking more of an interest in the business during the partnership. The second was allowing his emotional distress and his pride to prevent him from reaching out sooner to his friends (including me) to help him get things back on course. Instead, he found someone he hoped would fit into his old partner's shoes and blindly trusted that person to set up his showroom with no oversight. As amazing as his new creations were, the worst mistake of all was moving forward without a solid core structure underneath. Do some of these mistakes sound familiar? They should. Remember Phillip? He also blindly trusted someone to handle his business affairs, which eventually led to his downfall.

Ari's situation is all too common and one of the major reasons why I wanted to write this book. Too many people walk around with pretty business cards, fancy logos, voluminous business plans, colorful PowerPoint presentations, and glossy brochures and proclaim that they're ready for business. These make for a great first impression, but turn on the bright lamp and start the interrogation and you realize that the surface gloss doesn't go so deep. "What about the rest of it? Tell me how this is going to work. How much cash do you have? How long can you survive before you make your first sale?"

What I advised Ari to do is the same thing I did for myself when I started my own business. Once the ink on the corporate papers was dry,

I assembled my infrastructure team: an outside accountant, a lawyer, and an insurance agent. Then, I set up my books and made sure that I had a system in place that was prepared to deal with money once it started coming in. Last, I did what most people do as the first step: I opened a bank account.

Ari has followed through on my advice and is well on his way to becoming successful on his own. He's doing it the right way this time around.

CHAPTER 4

Garbage-in-Garbage-Out (GIGO)

"Garbage-in-garbage-out" (GIGO) is a term that I hope you never need to use. This dangerous practice has become increasingly common in the workplace as a result of shrinking budgets and insufficient staff. We are often led to believe that technology alone will solve all of our business problems, and there are plenty of vendors out there to sell you their latest wares with promises of overnight miracles. There are also many managers out there who are desperate to believe the false promises and don't do their own due diligence to see whether they make sense. These managers are often under extreme pressure to get a problem fixed quickly, and they don't have the tools or experience to know better. GIGO becomes very costly, and it is a good reason why my services are in demand, although I'd like to see this dangerous practice eliminated from the workplace vocabulary.

GIGO occurs when data is entered into an information system without regard for the quality. The end result is a bad report—garbage in—garbage out. Often this happens at the very start of a new system in an effort to "get it done" quickly. It has serious repercussions as a cascade of untrustworthy information triggers bad business decisions. The perpetrators of these situations make excuses and often try to deflect responsibility onto others through lies and deceit. GIGO also takes a negative toll on coworkers who must sort out and clean up the tangled mess—they can become stressed and confused, overwhelmed, unproductive, and very unhappy.

Let's face it: each of us faces the daily balancing act of pitting the things we love to do against the more boring and mundane tasks that we have to do. Most of us suck it up and get it done because we know that even the things we don't like to do are important and must be done with the same degree of quality as those we do like. Others are indifferent to the problems they cause by performing unpleasant tasks with less focus and quality than those that are pleasant. It falls to the managers to ensure that standards for quality are met at every stage of a project. This is especially true when it comes to entering data into a system.

Ann was a GIGO artist of the highest measure, a smooth talker who could charm her way out of a snake pit—and she had risen up the corporate ladder on the basis of a persona that exuded confidence and proficiency. Ann's story is worth telling because it is a good example of how common workplace problems are rooted and fermented in dysfunctional individual behavior. The more we are tuned in and sensitive to the detrimental effects of these misbehaviors around us, the better chance we have to avoid the associated pitfalls and to prevent problems from escalating.

As a senior manager, Ann delegated much of the day-to-day operations to her management team. She was more interested in establishing relationships that would further her career. By itself, this was not unusual. However, what was more insidious and harder to detect, and what complicated the situation, was that underneath the sugarcoated veneer, she was a highly unhappy and spiteful person with a venomous streak toward anyone who dared cross her.

To assert her authority and remove "obstacles" to her planned reorganization, Ann made some swift changes, reminiscent of the Queen of Hearts in *Alice in Wonderland* ("Off with his head!"). Quickly discharged were the specialists who managed the day-to-day data operations. She often used the "disaster of the day" as the justification for her decision. As the "old guard" was replaced, she brought in her own team—people who would do what she asked without question. You've heard of the NIH ("not invented here") principle? Ann's team exercised this principle in almost everything they did: any idea generated outside this newly established inner circle of managers was summarily dismissed without further discussion. However, it soon became clear that the new team didn't know what they were doing.

Ann's new job was to manage the information and communications infrastructure for her company's fifty thousand employees scattered around the country. Ann's team quickly focused their attention on an upgrade to a critical system. While the existing version was several versions behind the vendor's newest product, it still functioned effectively. So why on earth did Ann's group decide to throw out the existing version—which worked just fine—before the new version was ready? "The upgrade to the new version is fabulous and will solve all the problems we have with the current system," she announced with confident posturing to the higher-ups, who didn't know that the current system really had no problems.

In order to look good for her bosses, Ann created an unreasonable deadline for the upgrade. All parties involved, even the vendor of the new system version, told her that her deadline was impossible and the project would fail without adequate planning. Estimates ranged from twelve to eighteen months to implement the upgrade; instead, a three-month plan was implemented to upgrade "critical" functions, leaving the remainder for future phases (with no associated plan or schedule). A "fallback" plan, to restore the current version in case of problems with the new version, was proposed but immediately rejected. Her company exercised few checks and balances on her, until it was too late to repair the damage that was done.

What Ann neglected to tell her superiors was that the upgrade didn't really include all the "critical" functions. Several had been scheduled for a later phase, but no date was provided. "We'll worry about those components later," she told anyone who questioned the move. However, when the new version was deployed, it was severely limited by the lack of these components. To capture critical company data, Ann's team implemented a manual, paper-based process that was cumbersome and confusing and resulted in a paralyzed data entry process. Answers that were previously just a click away now required a ridiculous effort, if they could be found at all—a classic case of GIGO.

The people affected by this chaos became increasingly frustrated and angry, and customers began to talk of finding alternative sources for their support. Ann's staff was in constant crisis mode, not unlike a hospital emergency room, with cases prioritized by rank—who was screaming the loudest.

How did Ann get away with this? She thrived on chaos, subterfuge, and drama—smoke and mirrors—to cover up the real problems. When news of the problem leaked upward, she told her bosses, "We're getting to it," and she created another "short-term" and unrealistic deadline for her staff to meet. For each deadline, Ann's team created a superficial structure that appeared to be complete—until you looked under the hood. While Ann could point to the user interface with pride and show her bosses all the functions she had implemented, when the staff or customers tried to use the system, they were forced to create work-arounds, implemented to correct the shortcomings of the upgrade. Unfortunately, as long as this annoyance wasn't affecting the careers of her bosses, they paid little attention to the matter. Without recognition of the problem by the senior management, nothing was going to change.

Those forced to work under Ann had little choice other than to celebrate the little incremental short-term improvements they could make, the satisfaction of putting out the frequent fires, and knowing that were they not there to clean up the mess, matters would have been a thousand times worse. The staff adopted a strategy of conflict avoidance grounded in the fact that retribution was swift if there was even the slightest hint of disloyalty toward Ann. Most fell back on their patience, feeling that it was only a matter of time before the critical mass of Ann's misdeeds would catch up with her. Until then, survival and sanity depended on continuing simply to do the right thing, maintaining a paper trail to document the good work they did, and keeping things factual and objective.

It is an absurd, frustrating, and sometimes demoralizing predicament to work in a situation where nothing gets done and no one is willing to listen to those who have the solutions until things have deteriorated to a full-scale crisis. Many of those who worked for Ann faced the dilemma of remaining in their jobs or quitting. The best workers could—and often did—find other jobs, at a tremendous cost in legacy knowledge.

Truth be told, the monster that Ann had become was the creation of her senior management. Her fiefdom was the result of a major management faux pas, the failure to structure clear separation of duties. In her case, Ann's responsibilities should have been split between multiple parties for proper checks and balances. In addition, Ann's upper management didn't take action soon enough. While they knew about the problems, the solution was not going to be easy. As a result, they continued to ignore what was happening, failing to see the groundswell of discontent among staff and customers that was increasing on a daily basis.

Rather than accepting the status quo, staying the course, and hoping for the best—instead of acquiescing and tolerating this dysfunctional and destructive situation as "business as usual"—there is something that can be done on the front end to prevent it from happening in the first place. The solution can be described by one somewhat unpopular word: "planning." The sound of this word brings forth a bevy of excuses led by "We don't have the time." But what's the alternative? When you're asleep at the wheel, you'd better get ready for the inevitable crash. It's funny how people don't want to take the time to plan but seem to find plenty of time to deal with the resulting chaos afterward. "I've got to go put out this fire," overwhelmed and exasperated employees cry out. Every day, they routinely consume great amounts of energy when caught up in the busy, busy turmoil of the moment.

Once a big crisis leaves everything in rubble, decision makers are much more open to the idea of planning. Prevention, however, can be a hard sell. Motivating fast-moving people to put their routines on hold for a few days to devote the upfront time to planning and getting better organized is no easy task. Had Ann directed her team to create a realistic plan that met everyone's requirements and included a reasonable schedule, the project could have been successful. Had she fostered a team approach to the planning, she would have taken advantage of the skills of not only her own team but also the software vendor and the group that had supported the software before the upgrade. Had she convinced her management why and how upfront planning would save time and money in the long run instead of trying to make a quick impression, she would have received accolades from everyone. The few that go through the planning process see very quickly that the payoff is immediate. Taking the time to analyze the operations and increase efficiencies helps rid the workplace of this self-inflicted chaos and creates a comfort zone in its place. Everybody can move on with clearer and calmer heads to deal with the normal volatility of everyday life.

Did Ann's house of cards finally collapse? Yes, as usually happens in these sorts of situations. Customer complaints increased, and some customers began to talk of taking their support away from Ann's department. As these issues came to light and were not followed up by concrete actions to fix the problems, Ann's senior management began to see through her false promises and cover-ups. She wasn't fired, but actions were taken to limit the damage and increase pressure on her. Slowly but surely, Ann became more isolated. First, her managers restricted some of her key powers, including her authority to hire and fire people. "We've found you a wonderful new assistant, and she is reporting to us," her superiors decreed. "In fact, we will be meeting with her every week." In corporate etiquette, this act is a diplomatic way of putting Ann in a padded cell to quell any further possibility of damage. As a next step, they gave her a fancy new position as director of special projects. If you're ever given that title, don't get happy because what's in store is usually not considered a brilliant career move. Loosely translated, it means "Welcome to Siberia."

What lessons can we learn from Ann's example? Don't believe the hype. If something sounds too good to be true—as in implementing a major enterprise application in three months—it probably is and should be investigated. Don't live in an ivory tower. Don't rely just on information from direct reports, who may disclose only what they think the manager wants to hear. At any level, but especially at a senior level, where information must first flow through many layers of subordinates, a manager must have multiple lines of communication, including other managers, workers, and customers—checks and balances to ensure that hype is exposed before it becomes a problem. Don't have unrealistic expectations. Keep the best people around, and listen to what they have to say, even if it means more time. Ensure that there is adequate planning. As they say in the carpentry trade, "Measure twice; cut once"—it saves time and money in the long run. Don't be indifferent to what doesn't affect you directly. Don't wait for the problem to rise to your level; address it when it's small and you won't have to deal with it.

CHAPTER 5

Growing Pains

In the suburban countryside where I live, it's hard not to notice a curious development in recent times. Over rolling hills carpeted with pastures and woodlands and dotted with centuries-old farmhouses, new mansions of stone and glass have risen in the landscape. To say that they look a bit out of harmony with their surroundings is an opinion that not all may share, but I do. There's something even more curious about these grandiose homes when seen up close and inside. It's the bizarre sight of spaciously naked rooms without a single piece of furniture to be found. Yes, I'm talking about houses that are inhabited. I don't know why this is the case. Perhaps the people who live there simply don't need all the space or are taking extra time to do the interior decorating in stages. Or maybe the owners overspent on the edifice and didn't have the budget for anything else. Regardless, what is the point in building something so big only to have so many empty rooms? Just like a Hollywood set, it may look impressive and substantial from afar, but get closer and you'll see that it's not all it appears to be.

As you may have guessed, I live in one of those old farmhouses. It is one of life's great joys to come home after a hard day's work to a place you love. Unlike those of the new mansions, the rooms of my house are small and cozy, designed a long time ago when people were shorter in stature on average. Smaller rooms were also easier and less expensive to keep warm in the winter and cooler in the summer compared to the ballroom-sized living spaces of today. Although I have made one major improvement by upgrading to central air-conditioning, most everything else is as the builder intended a century and a half ago. The windows make a solid thud when closed, their longevity demonstrating the value of investing in quality. The wooden floors have a slight slope and creak with age but still bear that beautifully distinctive touch of a craftsman who had pride in his work. And, yes, there is furniture in each room that I have carefully chosen for functionality, comfort, and the kind of timeless style and quality that blend harmoniously with its space. I am fortunate because I truly couldn't ask for anything more. It is liberating and peaceful to be so content and not be trapped in the desire for more and more, bigger and better.

The metaphor about people building these big mansions but failing to make them fully functional and livable is like companies flaunting growth to the exclusion of quality. According to the media, size is the primary measure of success. Growth is what drives up stock prices. It is the yardstick that individuals use to measure how successful and important they are. Growth also determines the bonus at the end of the year—how many managers get bonuses for maintaining quality or their existing customer base by keeping their customers happy?

The tip-off to this "growth = success" mentality occurs when I first meet owners and key people within an organization and they immediately start bragging about their annual sales revenue, the number of employees, or their percentage of growth. The conversation usually starts off with, "I've grown eight hundred percent in the past two years. I'm making a hundred million dollars a year, and I've grown from fifty to five hundred people." They don't usually talk about the innovative work they're doing, employee satisfaction, or low staff turnover.

Once the chest thumping is over, I ask some pointed, detailed questions. "How is your cash flow? Can you pay your bills on time? While increasing your business, did you retain your existing client/customer base? Did you bring in forty new contracts, only to lose half of them? Did you match this growth with a corresponding growth in infrastructure, efficiencies, and capacity to handle it?"

Under this cross-examination, they change their body language. Legs and arms are suddenly crossed in a defensive pose. Their syllables become clipped and sentences curt. They can't understand why I'm not rolling over like everybody else, greasing their ego with how impressed I am. It's like they're only too willing to show me the big house as long as I don't peek inside through the windows—because inside there's only a card table and a folding chair and they're behind in the payments of the mortgage that they couldn't really afford.

When historians later come to examine the causes of America's economic woes in the early twenty-first century, I'm sure that many of them will single out this greedy obsession with growth, this form of instant gratification that has brought with it so many ruinous side effects. They will focus on the high-profile disasters such as Bernie Madoff, Enron, and some of the other high-stakes shell games and pyramid schemes and how they created the illusion of growth through moving money and commodities around in a convoluted web of deception. All that historical discussion is fine. But I'm more interested in how to prevent these kinds of situations, or at least expose them for what they are so we don't become their victims.

There is a similar pattern to companies that have this singular focus on growth. An experience I had with one company illustrates this pattern. Some time ago, I took on a subcontract with another company in an effort to continue one of our projects. We thought there would be synergy between their information technology experience and our business experience. Unfortunately, the synergy stopped there.

I agreed, although I knew that I was potentially compromising the autonomy I needed to ensure that my quality, reputation, and integrity couldn't be undermined. I laid out my basic terms to the other firm's vice president. My main concerns were keeping my existing staff employed on the project and getting paid on time. "If that is OK with you, then we are going to get along just fine," I said. A key element of this was retaining my project manager so that I'd have control over my portion of the project. The vice president agreed to my terms, and we began supporting the customer.

The problems started soon after, with a basic difference in company philosophy. It became clear that the other firm was interested primarily in rapid growth and the associated personnel counts and revenue. In the first month, there were multiple changes in personnel and points of contact as the company hired new people to accommodate its rapid growth. Each new person introduced another learning curve and delay, in addition to removing us from the person who had negotiated the terms of our agreement. As a result of all the staffing changes, the company had not submitted invoices to the customer, which caused a major delay in our getting paid. At this point, I realized that the firm was growing too quickly and wasn't expanding its internal infrastructure to support the additional work. New managers were hired but either didn't have the corporate knowledge or experience to make decisions or were so busy that they couldn't attend to everyone who needed them.

These problems escalated late one Sunday night, with a cryptic e-mail from the new senior vice president, Jim. "The project is taking a different direction now," he began. "The client agrees that we no longer need your manager, and we have now incorporated that position into our functioning team. As of next week, your contract management hours will be cut off. Thank you for facilitating the transition." I had never met Jim, and there had been no prior discussion with our previous points of contact that anything had changed. To say that I was shocked would be an understatement. I attempted to establish a meeting with Jim to discuss the situation but was told he was too busy and would not be able to meet for a few weeks. This was unacceptable, so I pressed, "Perhaps there is someone else in your company who can meet with us?" Jim reluctantly made time to meet the next day, Friday, not in the office but at Starbucks. I thought this was too public a location to discuss such sensitive issues, but I agreed to meet him there anyway.

Before we had barely exchanged introductions, he started his spiel. "I've been doing this a long time, and here's my philosophy about this business. Our company has grown from two million dollars to one hundred million in two years. The payment problem is just the result of growing pains, and I'm automating our internal processes with a system I've developed. We have big plans for this customer and are recommending a multimillion-dollar overhaul to its existing system. This is my area of expertise, and the customer is on board with this." I made it clear that I did not agree with his statements and I was willing to walk away from the project in accordance with my contract. This wasn't personal, but the relationship wasn't going to work out over time.

What Jim was trying to orchestrate was obvious. The reason we were in this situation was because his company wasn't monitoring its spending and was going to overrun the project budget unless something was immediately cut—and I was going to pay the price. I made it clear that if his company wouldn't honor its commitment, I would simply activate the termination clause of our subcontract. This made Jim very nervous; it would not look good for him to go back and tell his management that I was walking away. As the Starbucks meeting came to an end, he said that he would get back to me. Still, I saw the handwriting on the wall. Driving home, I thought, "This is not going to have a happy ending." However, I decided to take the long-term view and, for the good of the client, ride out the contract. In the end, the client recognized this typical pattern of behavior, and Jim's contract wasn't renewed. At the end of the day, his company's reputation was tarnished while mine was not.

I'm sure that Jim put his spin on what happened—saying that the client was going in a different direction—not caring that his company had not only lost a client and the income but also burned bridges and damaged its reputation in the process. A few more of these situations would further damage the company's reputation and undermine its ability to get new contracts. Rapid growth without proper infrastructure can kill a company. Maybe that's one explanation why some of those big mansions with empty rooms are going into foreclosure.

CHAPTER 6

The Cover-Up

The first summer camp that my parents sent me to as a small child had a no-frills method of teaching swimming. The camp counselor basically told us to jump into the pool and swim. I guess I could have informed him that I didn't know how to swim, but I didn't. Perhaps my fear of being seen as inept and standing apart from the crowd was greater than my fear of drowning. So, what did I do? I tossed myself into the water, and I playacted at swimming. I stood upright and frantically paddled across the pool the best I could, and, fortunately, I didn't drown. To some, it may have appeared that I was swimming, but I wasn't. The next summer, I went to another (more expensive) camp, where they actually taught me how to swim.

At your workplace, chances are good that there are one or more prototypes of the camp counselor and Little Nancy lurking about. It's the case of management wishfully thinking that someone with little or no experience and training will float along trouble free and not sink. These pretend swimmers drift along and find creative ways to make it appear that they can "handle it" because they are afraid that if they fess up, they will be fired—and in most cases, they are probably right. It is easier for the managers to find another floater than to change their criteria and practices, which only perpetuates the problem.

Val's story is a classic case of the over-her-head-fly-by-the-seat-of-her-pants-and-cover-her-tracks syndrome. Val was the manager of a small division within an information technology company. This division had a stellar reputation for delivering quality products and the latest technologies. Val was technically competent, well versed in all of the latest technology upgrades, and able to train her staff on how to promote the newest products. She had been performing well on the job as a technology expert under the division leader for several years. Her division leader was also technically competent but without business skills. Think of her manager as the camp counselor but with one important difference—he didn't know how to swim, either. It is important to note that neither Val nor her boss was a sinister or nasty person. In fact, both of them were personable and friendly and had no malice or bad intentions.

When the company decided to decentralize the business operations, Val immediately stepped forward to set up the business structure for her division, with her boss thinking, "Oh, great! I have someone on my staff who can take care of this for me! Let her run with it."

The fatal flaw was that Val and her boss were asked to do something that was new territory and they weren't provided the tools to do it. They weren't trained, and they were expected to be able to swim on the first day. So, to stretch this metaphor further, both Val and her boss had jumped into the same pool. It is one thing to know what you don't know, but it becomes an out-of-control mess when you don't know what you don't know. So it is hard to ask for help as things begin to deteriorate if you don't have a clue that you are having a problem.

The big problem was that Val knew absolutely nothing about business operations, and neither did her boss. As a result, the division started to bleed. First and foremost, Val was asked to figure out how to price the new products, including the device costs, plus a percentage needed to cover the overhead of running the division and staff. However, she didn't have a clue about how to go about this, so she added what she thought the customer would be willing to pay. Her boss, thinking that she knew what she was doing, went along with Val's recommendations. Little thought was given to the financial impact of adding staff if the situation warranted. They didn't realize that every time a new employee used a paper clip, let alone drew salary, more red ink was being added to the bottom line. Instead of turning a handsome profit, her division saw its deficit growing with every passing month.

How did this so easily escape detection? It stayed hidden for a short while because the company had an abundant cash cow in another department. With all the money rolling in from the other department, Val's miscalculations in coming up with accurate cost models and getting timely bills out to the customers fell under the radar. Think of it like the recording industry of the 1970s and '80s. If they had Michael Jackson selling millions of albums, who cared if they took exorbitant losses rolling the dice on new artists? Those were the bygone good old days. But as fortunes in the world of commerce can be fickle, cash cows can and do dry out. When that happened at Val's company, the spotlight quickly shifted to Val's department, and the scrutiny began—and that is the point at which I was called in by Val's boss to stop the bleeding. Her boss was very smart, and once he realized he had a problem—and realized the extent of the problem—he moved quickly to find a solution. Just like Ann's situation before, it had to rise to a crisis point first before corrective action was initiated.

What made the situation even more chaotic was the competency level of the employees working under Val. She did not know how to hire people appropriate for business operations. Without proper training, direction, or organizing structure from the top, her team tried the best they could and worked conscientiously. However, good intentions were not enough to make the business operate profitably.

Once I got there, I quickly realized that there were a number of problems in addition to the bleeding. A major problem was the skill level of the staff. Because Val didn't understand the job requirements, she didn't know what skills were needed on her team. She also tended to hire based on friendships, personality, and other reasons unrelated to the job requirements. In addition, there was no formal training because Val didn't know what was needed.

Another major problem was the lack of cross-training. If someone was on vacation, was out sick, or quit, it therefore became a major crisis, and the work came to a complete standstill. The loss of any one person could cripple the organization. This also gave the employees power over their boss, which some exploited. There is one highly effective way to prevent this predicament from ever gaining traction. It's called cross-training, a well-known concept—but one that you unfortunately don't see very often in the workplace because it requires effort to make it happen. In a nutshell, cross-training eliminates the single points of failure because every employee has someone else who is qualified to step in and do his or her job if necessary. In Val's world, everyone was a single point of failure because nobody was watching while each was off doing his or her own thing.

Cross-training, like that dreaded concept called planning, is another nuisance on that woeful list with painful dentistry that nobody initially wants to do. Added to it is the natural aversion most coworkers initially have to the process. Getting over this hump often requires the boss or supervisor to get involved and be physically present, like a hovering elementary school teacher. Here's a surefire motivator: "Guess what? You're not going on vacation until you've trained your backup." The barriers then start to break down, sped along with the thought of that waiting bottle of Corona and slice of lime on the sandy beach.

It doesn't take long before both parties learn a surprising value to cross-training. A transformation starts when employees begin connecting the dots between their little piece of the action and how it affects a person on the other side of the office—and everybody else for that matter. In addition, there are other more subtle benefits. There's a better sense of communication and cohesion, and the operations seem to flow more efficiently. Egos are also held in check. No one wields that sword of invincibility, holding his or her boss hostage, saying, "You can't fire me because no one else can do my job."

Make no mistake: it does require a lot of time, effort, and expense up front to do it right. For that reason, a company that has effectively cross-trained teams seems more the exception than the rule. The idea of having to make that front-end investment often runs contrary to the penny-wise, cost-cutting mentality at most companies today.

Companies (such as mine) that make the commitment to this practice see how their enterprise stands out among the competition in productivity and ultimately in high customer satisfaction and retention.

If you're still not convinced, here are the dividends resulting from cross-training that I've experienced in my company: turnover has gone way down due to employee satisfaction and growth; the customers have people available to get work done when others are on vacation; and when someone quits, it's no big deal—we can take on the additional workload and tasks with minimal increased costs to the customers.

Val's manager brought me in to do a study of the operation and to determine whether they were doing the right thing. The manager didn't feel comfortable with the current situation because he wasn't getting any financial reports and his managers were asking him questions he couldn't answer. When the manager presented my proposal to his managers, they balked at the cost and the need for this evaluation. He fought to bring me in, and he won that battle. He didn't know it at the time, but this was a career-saving move on his part.

The mentality of his management was that infrastructure costs were unnecessary and should be minimized. They felt that the programmatic costs were far more important to the organization and required little or no justification. My first recommendation was to stabilize and build the necessary infrastructure to support the complexity of this operation. With proper infrastructure, Val's manager could sleep at night because he was getting regular reports and financial projections to ensure that they remained in the black and could make sound business decisions.

So what happened to Val? Shortly after I arrived on the scene, she left the company for a job more aligned with her real talents and skills. What happened to the division manager? He became a hero in the company for recognizing the need for change and implementing the necessary systems and controls before the division became insolvent. Because he recognized the problem and was strong enough to take the steps to fix it, he was able to turn things around before it was too late. As a result, when he retired a few years later, he received his company's highest reward for his contribution to the success of his division.

CHAPTER 7

Let the Games Begin

Many of today's workplaces have become battle zones. Most people would say this is caused by increased competition among managers for dwindling resources, the result of cost cutting in an economic downturn. However, another more deeply underlying problem pervades society and particularly the modern business world. Workplace battles are often caused by the selfish behavior of individuals who are more concerned with their own career growth than with making sound business decisions. Company loyalty is thrown out the window in exchange for personal gain; workers no longer see any benefit to working together on the same team and spend most of their energy on how they can quickly get ahead. Managers and ambitious employees look for the "quick win" that will gain them recognition, bonuses, promotions—and the increased status that goes along with them.

Add in today's challenging economy and the increased focus on belt tightening and the situation becomes even more pervasive. It's dog-eat-dog, with turf wars at every turn—and may the strongest one win. The battles take a huge toll on the organization as a whole and all the people who work within it. Too often, the politically motivated actions of these individuals exacerbate the situations they were supposed to remedy.

Belt tightening can be a good thing when it forces us to identify the true sources of inefficiencies and waste, a review that companies should conduct on a regular basis. However, too often companies make across-the-board cost-cutting decisions without looking at program efficiencies and strike with a broad and indiscriminate stroke. This can result in cutting necessary infrastructure rather than a failing pet program. Planning and training costs, which become more important with fewer resources, are often the first items targeted to be cut.

This behavior follows a familiar pattern. In an attempt to reduce costs, internal staffing is cut, but management expects equal performance from the remaining employees. The training budgets are slashed or removed entirely. Consequently, work becomes rushed, corners are cut, and attention to detail is thrown out the window. Quality drops, resulting in lost sales, and the cycle repeats itself.

Enter Dave, hired as a new manager to take over a division that was mired in problems, including terrible morale and unhappy customers. In the interview, confident Dave assured the manager that he could "fix the place in thirty days." What Dave's boss failed to tell him was that he would have no access to his predecessor, and he was inheriting a disgruntled deputy who had applied for Dave's job and didn't get it. Dave now had to deal with Linda, who was uncooperative to an extreme. Linda had good reason to resent Dave from the start. She had been acting in his position for a number of months and felt slighted when she wasn't promoted to his job. "I'm not getting anything out of this, and I'm not respected, so why should I care?" was her attitude. "I'll just do what I need to do to get by until something better comes up." It was a recipe for underperformance and a no-win situation.

The only thing that they seemed to do well was attack each other. Linda had the institutional knowledge to be an asset to Dave, but because of her attitude, she refused to help him. She constantly undermined him with the employees and customers with comments like, "Since Dave has so much great experience, he should be able to answer that question." Linda could have helped Dave and become a valuable asset to her new boss. Unfortunately—for both of them—she drew her battle lines and initiated the first attacks.

Dave realized very quickly that he couldn't count on Linda, so he brought in his own team, selected for their previous loyalty to him. However, they quickly became overwhelmed because they didn't know what they were doing and Linda was doing nothing to help them. Dave got back at Linda by assigning a lot of his work to her, but she spent most of her energy on finding another job and using up her leave balance. As a result, Dave became increasingly frustrated and began to lash out at others to divert attention from his own problems. His new people tried to protect him by blaming everything on Linda and her people. The clash of egos between the two factions continued as skirmishes were won and lost.

For a while, these conflicts languished in a state of deadlock—like trench warfare, where neither party seems to give an inch. At this point, Dave and Linda had something in common: a bad attitude. The job goals they had set out to accomplish became secondary as they went into survival mode, hanging on as long as they could in a war of attrition, with Linda hoping her boss would leave or she would find another job and Dave hoping that Linda would leave so he could be free of her undermining actions.

Where was Dave's boss during all of this? In most cases, unless the shrapnel strikes uncomfortably close to the executive office, there is no meaningful intervention from senior management. After all, their policies created the mess to begin with. Most of the time, they let the turf battles play themselves out because eventually—and virtually without fail—one of the combatants is going to win and the loser will move on. In our story, as is true in most cases, the one who didn't get the job (Linda) is usually the one who has to leave.

To be blunt, Dave's boss should have intervened and prevented the situation from spiraling downward. After all, Linda was a valuable employee, but she was never made to feel valued. In fact, although she had interviewed for Dave's position, her boss didn't have the decency to give her any feedback. To make it worse, she found out that she didn't get the job in a group meeting with all of the other employees. Despite her in-depth knowledge and skill in her position, she didn't receive any recognition at all. Isn't it the boss's job to say, "Linda, you didn't get the job, but we're going to do this for you instead"? Dave's boss could also have separated the combatants once the battle began—something as simple as transferring Linda to a new post. Instead, he left her hanging in an unacceptable situation. Even with a more respectful approach, Linda likely would have left the company anyway, but she might have been more positive and cooperative in her final days.

Another common battle occurs when management pits the sales, marketing, and product management employees against their back office "admin" colleagues. Usually, the workers in the back office are the underdogs, taking the first hit in the popular cost-cutting area of "overhead." "I've cut ours to ten percent of our costs," one manager boasts. Another counters, "Ours is down to eight percent." The next adds, "We've gotten ours down to four cents on the dollar." Numbers are thrown around like buzzwords, and nobody knows what they mean anymore. Ten percent of what? This mentality seems to be everywhere, especially in the arena of nonprofits competing for your charitable dollars. They flaunt their reduced overhead expenses to inspire confidence that the lion's share of the donations are reaching their intended beneficiaries.

It's not a bad thing to rein in outrageous overhead costs such as excessive CEO salaries and bonuses and other company "perks." But a certain amount of overhead is vitally important to sustain the infrastructure of the organization and to ensure proper checks and balances. Cutting too much in this area can have devastating consequences. But what's the point if ninety-five cents of your dollar to feed that starving child ends up on the black market because there is no one on the ground to administer it properly?

The same principle applies to our for-profit organizations and governmental institutions. In the current frenzy, far too many cut overhead well below the quick and to the degree that efficient, secure, and chaos-free operations can no longer be sustained. It's easier—and very tempting—to take the knife to "overhead" because it is not a popular or sexy endeavor. It's also far easier for the senior executives to target overhead rather than execute the politically sensitive job of uncovering the sources of waste on the product side. The people marketing and producing the widgets and closing the big sales are the ones who get bonuses and awards at the end of the year. Those who help run a tight ship rarely get such reward or recognition.

Turf wars between the program office and overhead staff occur because no one is focusing on what is right or what is really needed for the company. Company owners are asleep at the wheel and allow program department staff to sling mud at the overhead staff and vice versa. What is needed to rise above this predicament is obvious. You, as an employee, must recognize your value to the team and perform your work to the best of your ability—regardless of what happens around you. Don't participate in the skirmishes and battles. This means occasionally swallowing your pride. However, in the long run, your consistency and professionalism will pay off.

Despite the fact that what I do for a living is considered "overhead," I have always looked for ways to operate more efficiently, and as a result, I have earned the respect of both my bosses and the program staff. When you create an effective area of business, people will usually respect it and give you your space. Given the degree of dysfunction in most businesses, you will stand out as a shining example of a part of your organization that is not in continuous damage control mode.

In the end, to avoid getting stuck in a battle zone, you must build trust by bringing your "A" game to the job every day, showing your true value to others by achieving results, and keeping your head down and out of the fray. Nevertheless, if faced with an unavoidable budget cut, you should be clear and stand firm. "I understand you have a budget situation. Understand that I'm not realistically going to be able to do the same level of work for that money. Something has to give. Understand that I have a job that needs to be done and a good reputation I'd like to keep. We need to meet in the middle, or I will have to walk away."

CHAPTER 8

Smoke and Mirrors

"If it looks too good to be true, it probably is." This is one of my favorite sayings because it describes one of the leading causes of the nonsense I deal with day in and day out. What keeps me so busy is a direct result of the fact that Americans are the undisputed world masters of spin. We know how to put on a good show regardless of whether there's real substance behind it. We say the things we think our target audience wants to hear. We dress our data up in beautiful PowerPoint presentations with fancy graphs and slick-looking diagrams. And as listeners, we want to believe that all we see and hear is true, like small children who love fairy tales with happy endings.

We read in the news about the more dramatic cases of con men and women in business, the Ponzi schemes, and various forms of creative accounting that move assets around to make companies look more profitable. We ask, "How could it be that so many bright investors could be taken in by such falsehoods?" We shake our heads in disbelief at coworkers who claimed not to know what was going on and felt equally deceived. Weren't they smart people, too?

Most of us deal with much more minor situations at our own jobs—which nonetheless can create a lot of damage. The case of Brent is a classic in demonstrating just how easy it is to milk the system and to get ahead based on the outward veneer and not on actual substance. In terms of appearance, Brent was first-rate in that department. A manager at a high-tech firm, he was tall, good looking, and well dressed, and he had a winning smile. He presented himself with an air of confidence and sophistication, and he walked into the room like he owned it.

Such was the persuasive power of his personality that he could manage to convince people to follow his lead. "This is how I did it in my last job," he would tell his upper management to get them to go along with his ideas. His biggest accomplishment in this regard was getting his boss to agree to dismantle one of the cardinal rules of sound financial management. The separation of operations and finance is there for good reason. Brent's idea was to oversee both functions within his division so that he could operate more efficiently.

But it was really about Brent and his ego; he didn't want to be held accountable, he didn't like his actions to be questioned, and he didn't like ideas that didn't originate with him. "I came here to simplify things, and the finance team is making everything complicated," Brent told me. "I don't want to spend a lot of money on accounting, and I don't need all of these reports. I'm going to bring in someone to show them how it should be done, and I can achieve significant cost savings by doing it my way."

Brent brought in someone to dismantle the financial controls within his division. He made it her mission, and her performance evaluation depended on her success. She was a smart person, but she was set up to fail from the outset by being incentivized to do something that would ultimately have negative consequences. She was quite popular with Brent and his management as she set about to systematically remove the financial controls.

Fortunately, Brent's financial team had built a solid foundation of competence and trust throughout the company. The CFO and the financial group worked together behind the scenes to prevent any permanent damage. The financial group created a clear paper trail for every action and reported all irregularities directly to the CFO. The CFO established new procedures and policies to block inappropriate actions from Brent's office. At one point, new policies and directives were being issued on a weekly basis.

This situation split the organization into two factions and became very uncomfortable for the financial group. Brent suspected there was collaboration but was powerless to do anything about it, which infuriated him. He used his assistant to torment the financial group and bombard them with requests to change the financial structure. The financial team would prepare elaborate reports for Brent's reorganization requests, knowing that they would be rejected by the CFO's office. This cycle of requests and rejections went on for almost a year, wearing everyone down in the process. Eventually, Brent's boss left the company and was replaced by someone with more business experience who recognized immediately that Brent's oversight of the financial group was highly inappropriate because it defeated the rule of checks and balances. After a year of making life hell for everyone, Brent was gone.

Ultimately, Brent failed because there were people in his company who were smart enough to see through his charisma and who understood the basics of sound business organization. Unfortunately, this is not always the case, as illustrated by the unfortunate investors who listened to and believed the promise of financial riches that would come from following the advice of Bernie Madoff.

CHAPTER 9

Survival of the Fittest

In case you haven't gotten the message while reading these pages so far, much of what makes people miserable on the job comes from having to deal with miserable people. Way too much of our energy and productivity is squandered by conflict and infighting. The amount of time employees devote to attacking others or defending themselves from attacks can be massive.

To the observer, these conflicts almost always appear smooth and relatively peaceful on the surface. In fact, we rarely see two wild dogs getting bloody going after the same bone. Instead, people usually play nice but do most of the damage terrorizing each other in more circuitous and non-confrontational ways. Together, we're all friends and having what appears to be a garden party. In reality, everything is done behind your back, and the damage usually happens so fast that you won't see it coming unless you have your radar up.

Personally, if there's going to be conflict, I prefer it to be in the open. For that reason, I respected Brent. Even though he made my life hell for a year (and taught me a lot in the process), at least he had the guts to tell me to my face that he couldn't stand me. In our nation's capital, where I work, there's a funny expression to describe this: "A Washington friend is someone who stabs you in the chest." Of course, President Truman would have questioned whether such a thing even existed. He was famous for saying "if you want a friend in Washington, get a dog."

I can't say that I was always so skillful with handling people with bad intentions. It took me a while to figure it out, but I've had plenty of practice over the years and have honed my craft. Being that my job is to uncover malpractice, I encounter my fair share of these sorts of people, who often regard me as their nemesis. With the years, I have gotten even better at sniffing out potential mean-spirited people before they have a chance to get out their knives. Here's one litmus test. If that person freely and gratuitously offers up personal attacks on coworkers past and present and talks trash about the boss, chances are good you've got a certified problem child on your hands.

The blue ribbon winner among all the mean-spirited people I have ever encountered was Laura. I'm not a psychologist, so I won't even begin to speculate on what possessed her to behave the way she did. But what was obvious, and what she shared as a common denominator with all the other nasty people who were messing up in positions of power, was the simple fact that she was in way over her head. She knew there was something seriously wrong with the department she oversaw, but she didn't want anybody to see it. So, she pointed the blaming finger at others, including me. Like Brent, she could turn on the charm and talk a good game when the situation called for it. The transformation between the charismatic smooth talker and her very unhappy nature and hateful demeanor was dramatic and almost cinematic, conjuring images of the sneering, mean-hearted doll Chucky in the *Child's Play* horror movies.

She was a master of the smoke-and-mirrors game and creative in making up all sorts of stories to discredit me when the truth of her mismanagement started coming out. If new people came into the organization, they would have already heard from her all sorts of horrible things about me before I had the chance to meet them. Laura was not going to go away anytime soon, so I had to find a way to work with her.

Dealing with Laura and any other mean-spirited person involves following some general rules of engagement. After successfully implementing these tips, I move into a more specialized and strategic approach to clean things up. But first, here are these preliminary golden rules:

Don't make it personal. Be respectful. Never raise your voice. Even if you're angry, stay cool. Many mean-spirited people thrive on conflict, and the more heated it becomes, the more enjoyment they seem to derive. Getting you to lose your cool becomes a victory for these people and makes them feel more powerful. Seeing you upset and discombobulated may give them a misguided sense of justification that they're right and you're wrong. When I was behaving badly as a kid, my father used this tip to great effect. His calm and quiet demeanor communicated his disapproval and disappointment in me a hundred times more powerfully than if he had he lashed out.

Stick to the facts. "Just the facts, ma'am" was the mantra associated with the actor Jack Webb as Sergeant Friday on the classic old television series *Dragnet*. His dialogue was kept sparse, clipped, and understated when he was investigating a crime. Follow his lead by trying to keep things factual when it comes to work-related matters. Importantly, do not volunteer any information about yourself outside of work, such as your habits and lifestyle, what you did the previous weekend, or what you are planning to do for your holiday. On the other hand, you are free to engage others with questions such as "How did your weekend go?" or "Did you play tennis?" But trust me: someone who is stabbing you in the back will look to twist any data you offer about yourself into fodder for the innuendo and character assassination mill.

Limit your engagement with your adversary and keep the paper trail going. It's a given that you should keep your integrity at all times, but sometimes that's not enough. Maintaining a paper trail that documents your actions and interactions is one of the best preventions and defenses against mean-spirited people. It also helps if you try to limit your face time with a person like Laura as much as possible and don't go out of your way to seek her out. Remember that everything you do directly with her without a witness can be twisted, fabricated, or even turned into something she will claim never happened. It can get ridiculous. Along with always keeping a third party involved in your interactions, keep those e-mail memos flowing that summarize events and actions taken. That way you'll have real-time collaborating evidence and won't be helpless when the "he-said-she-said" game begins.

Always take the high road. Never speak disparagingly about the mean-spirited person to others. If you do, you are starting to go down that slippery slope to becoming a mean-spirited person yourself. It's not OK if I say "You're not going to believe what Laura did!" Don't sugarcoat the situation, but emphasize the issue and not the perpetrator. Compare "The matter about the overhead is going to come up at the meeting" and "Laura's screw-up with the budget is going to come up at the meeting." It's not the time to bad-mouth Laura and get my digs in. Most of my coworkers are probably going to know, but if they ask questions such as "Would that person be Laura?" let them bring her name up rather than making it obvious that I'm making a personal attack on Laura. It's OK to answer them truthfully—"Yeah, I think so." The other part of taking the high road is to avoid the mean behavior of blaming others for your mistakes. As an imperfect human being, I make mistakes all the time—but hopefully not the same one twice. Own up to your mistakes quickly and honestly and promise they won't happen again so they don't become liabilities.

Even if you follow all these rules, you will still have to be on damage control alert at all times. You may find out that disparaging information, from rumors to outright personal attacks, has been spread about you with the intent to seriously damage your reputation. The longer you wait before taking action, the worse matters can become. Here again, the operative strategy is to be subtle, sensitive, truthful and maintain your integrity. The idea is not to take drastic action to make it look obvious that you're on the defensive. Again, in this situation, I want to make sure that my message is heard so people will come to their own conclusions and understand that what Laura is saying about me is patently not true.

One situation with Laura got particularly bad when she misrepresented in an e-mail that a crucial deadline was missed for filing a report because my group had dropped the ball. Her intent was to try to get me fired over this matter. Some of the people in the organization who were loyal to me tipped me off about her accusations. What complicated matters more was that the person in power Laura had tried to poison against me was Peter, someone with whom I had very little interaction.

What helped in this predicament was the fact that I made it a daily practice to walk the corridors to check in on my employees, so there were natural opportunities to meet or run into Peter. In the same way, if I had received an e-mail from Peter on an unrelated matter, it would likewise be a chance to engage him and be helpful. Again, with this type of damage control, it is important not to be overanxious and pounce. If there were not a natural context in which to talk about the matter with Peter during the first meeting, I would let it go and wait until the second, third, or even fourth opportunity.

Keeping your energy clean and being confident, self-assured and not defensive in this interaction will more often than not let someone like Peter know that you have nothing to hide. In this particular situation, it made it very comfortable for Peter to bring the matter up himself after exchanging pleasantries or talking about a nonrelated business matter. "Nancy, I got an e-mail from Laura, and I talked to her team about this," he volunteered. "Yes, I talked to them, too," I answered, devoid of any condescending attitude or negativity. Then, Peter put his cards down on the table and started to speak negatively about Laura himself, as if he saw through the situation. "Yes, I know they were saying it was my fault that it didn't happen. I felt bad that you didn't get that report when you needed, and I wish I could have helped," I said. I explained to him the logistics of how my group had delivered, but the missing information came from a part where I had no involvement or control. "Yes, we really need to work together to fix this situation," he concluded.

The moral of this particular story is that if a person is being mean to you, there's a good chance that he or she is also being equally nasty to others. You're probably not the only one suffering by being around this person. Follow these rules and keep on the high road. Before you know it, you'll come in one day and discover a memo that today is Laura's last day.

CHAPTER 10

Betrayal and Trust

I had to go into Tom's office at a telecom company and tell him the bad news that his right-hand person was incompetent and had created a lot of damage. This is why my job is not just about analyzing numbers and systems but also dealing with the human drama not far underneath it all. It is hard to predict how someone is going to react to betrayal. He stood for a few moments in stunned silence, shaking his head, after being informed by the project manager that there would be a substantial loss this year. "I trusted her," he said, not hiding the intensity of his disappointment. Coming to his senses, he realized that it was not personal; she hadn't intentionally set out to destroy him, but a second after giving him the news, their relationship was forever damaged. Such a devastating loss of trust awakens the fear of the unknown: "What else did she not tell me?" It's a terrible feeling of helplessness and loss of control within the organization.

Tom's assistant wasn't going to tell him that she didn't have the right background for the position, and she had come with good references. Years ago, a reference meant something and would prevent someone from misrepresenting his or her skills. Perhaps the tide shifted when employers were suddenly instructed by their lawyers to give out only basic information when asked. "I'm not going to give you a bad reference because you'll sue me" has become the prevailing attitude. So, any misdeeds at an old job don't often follow people as they float on to the next stop. It is incumbent on the part of the hiring manager to clearly understand the requirements of the job and to be able to evaluate the new hire's performance. Failure to do so can be catastrophic to your operation, as the story of Tom and his assistant shows.

I don't rely on others to tell me how things are going. I am visible; I walk the halls and engage my own employees every day. By doing so, I am building with them the very foundation for trust. Trust is not a given but has to be earned over time. For example, some say negatively that I "micromanage" my employees. They ask me, "Why are you down here? Why aren't you off in your ivory tower?" "At the end of the day, it's my name on this company and not yours," I answer. "That's why I'm watching over your shoulder until I am at a point where I can trust you." If somebody tells me that he or she has done something, I am going to look at it and verify that it has been done. After the eighteenth time, I know I can trust that person. "Prove to me that it's true," I will say. If the person is right, then we won't have a problem. The ones who are wrong will get very nervous and defensive and will show attitude. The same principle applies to building trust with clients: after the eight hundredth time of saying "This is the truth" and seeing it verified as correct, a precious and unshakable bond of trust is created between my customer and me.

That bond can be an early warning system against betrayal. Susan, a former boss whose job I had helped save, had come back some years later and decided she wanted to steal my client. She tried to send out damaging rumors that there was dissatisfaction with my work and my contract was on shaky ground. What she didn't consider was the trust factor. The people she talked to immediately came to me and quickly exposed what she was up to. Instead of becoming a big disaster, it turned into a comedic farce. For example, on a few occasions I came face-to-face with Susan in the lunchroom or in a hallway. She was clearly nervous in not knowing whether I was aware of what she was trying to do. I made pleasant small talk with her. There was nothing to be gained by confronting her directly. Think of it this way: when you see a rabid dog, do you confront the dog? With both the dog and a betrayer, you're usually not dealing with anything rational. The exception to that is when people are less blatant and more marginal in their misdeeds—in that case I can possibly turn them around. Those people I will confront.

By not confronting Susan directly, I refused to throw more fuel on the fire. Because that kind of person thrives on drama and tries to twist these situations into her favor, there's nothing to be gained by playing that game. It comes down to that old adage about keeping your friends close but your enemies closer. Keep taking the high road. Whether you like it or not, you're going to have to deal with that person again. It can feel like being in a small town. Susan may go over to a competitor. In her case, it was easy because everyone knew what she was doing. Competition is fair and healthy when it is based on our talents and the results of our work, but Susan had a less than stellar history of accomplishment that rested on the backs of others. Nobody likes a parasite. Susan's coworkers got so angry at what she was doing that I just stood by as they became more and more disgusted. Before long, she vaporized.

When the betrayers are employees, it requires the patience of a chess player. Again, as with Susan, I usually avoid direct confrontation and bide my time. Moving my pieces around the board, I surround betrayers with good people. Pretty soon, they get lonely and isolated. They're neutralized to the point that the damage they can create is minimal. Then, at the first natural opportunity to let them go, like a budget cut, they're gone.

One decisive way to prevent betrayal is by creating the kind of positive workplace environment that is hard to beat. So many times, I will meet a former employee who was lured away by what he or she thought would be a more lucrative, high-powered advancement with another company. The former colleague usually becomes quite nostalgic about some of the nicer things he or she once had but lost.

PART II

Rising above
the Dysfunction

CHAPTER 11

Redeeming the Disposable Employee

A woman I know came into her office recently and was greeted by security. They told her that they were there to immediately escort her out of the building, barely giving her the dignity of a few moments to collect her personal belongings. I don't know whether she was the perfect employee, but despite twenty years of service, she was deemed disposable and no longer a fit with the culture of her company. Along with the few things she could carry, she was also walking out the door with two decades of expertise on the job, a valuable asset that nobody bothered or cared to consider.

Life is not always fair, as every child learns. But few things infuriate me more than the injustice of seeing the wrong person terminated and another wrong person rewarded. Add this high on the list of the peeves that motivated me to start my own company. Let's face it—there are no perfect employees. We each have our quirks and eccentricities, our room for improvement. If you can't handle dealing with quirky people, guess what? You will be in for a frustrating future.

What prevails in most companies today is a body shop mentality. If a problem comes up with a person and his or her performance, more often than not very little effort is given to working through the issues. The decision maker looks at how messy and time-consuming it is to talk sense into this person and how much more expeditious it is just to hand out a pink slip and find a replacement.

I am willing to work with anyone who shows a willingness to try to improve. I can handle an occasional bad attitude with generally conscientious work. If people are willing to work on their problems and show progressive improvement, then I'm not going to give up on them. However, if employees continually show attitude or are disrespectful, I will show them the door without hesitation.

The story I'm about to share with you is a shining example of the diamonds you can find buried in the landfill of disposable employees. Yes, I did have to get a little dirty in the digging, but the ultimate reward is satisfying in a way no superlatives can begin to adequately express.

As I glanced over Penny's résumé, I thought, "This candidate looks really great, and she has all the right background." That impression continued during the job interview. Penny showed up for the meeting impeccably dressed in a nice suit. What I later learned was that she had bought it at a thrift store for ten dollars because she didn't have the money to buy a new one. Penny always looked professional and never once complained about having to wear business attire in hot weather. She was articulate and respectful, and I hired her on the spot. "I appreciate the opportunity," she told me earnestly at the end of the interview.

Within a short time of her coming on board, a different and much less favorable side of Penny began to show itself. She had very obvious anger issues triggered by strong ideas about integrity. Wherever she saw waste and abuse, she became righteous and rigid and would mouth off both to coworkers and in front of clients. Over the smallest details, she would explode in a fit of anger.

A chorus of coworkers urged me to fire Penny. However, I could get along and communicate with her and vice versa, and I saw something special in her. Her work was brilliant despite the turbulence around her. But I could see something wild and untamed in her eyes. As the complaints about Penny mounted, I dug in deeper to defend her. "If she goes, I go, so get over it," I countered when the criticism got especially fierce.

When Penny became agitated, I would take her aside and get her settled down. "Do you hear what I'm saying to you?" I would repeat until I was assured that she finally understood what I was saying. What gave me optimism was that I began to see incremental improvement. Some part of what I would say to her each time seemed to stick. "OK, if that part sank in, maybe I can get a little bit more if I try again," I thought.

It wasn't my imagination that a shift was occurring because coworkers began to notice a huge difference. "Something's happened; something's changed," they would say to me. "I'm getting along with her now. She's not mouthing off to anybody anymore."

The transformation in Penny had an unexpected bonus. It sent out positive waves among her coworkers. They might have questioned my sanity at first, but they witnessed firsthand that there was a method to my madness, and with a little extra effort, we got beyond the problems. It underscored for them that because I wasn't going to give up on Penny and throw away all her talent and potential, maybe I would also be there in that same way for the rest of them, too.

Penny still has a little outburst from time to time, but it is nothing to worry about any longer. Everybody has some baggage. In the end, it boils down to putting people into situations that harness their strengths and avoiding those that feed into their issues. So, if someone like Penny is at risk of mouthing off, I don't put her directly in front of the customer or the sales force. At the end of the day, Penny is incredibly smart and extremely loyal. In fact, she is anything but disposable. She is indispensable and one of my most valuable resources.

CHAPTER 12

Taking the Test

W hat I love is when an amazingly simple and profound answer suddenly appears to solve a problem that had once seemed insurmountable. In this particular case, out of adversity came the gift that keeps on giving. What emerged from this situation is nothing short of a vaccine for a good number of the problems discussed in this book. Armed with this resource, we can reduce some of the most significant causes of waste and unrealized potential—and, yes, even failure. What's more, the process happens quickly before a new employee even comes in for the first day of work.

The particular problem that sparked all of this happened within the very company I had worked so hard to build into a viable enterprise—my own. Deteriorating conditions on the job got to be so bad that I basically wanted to walk away. I went so far as to contact my accountant and tell him point-blank that I wanted out. "Can I sell the business?" I asked him. He tried hard to mask his disbelief that I wanted to exit so abruptly. It was as if I suddenly announced that after a few years of motherhood, I had a change of heart and wanted to put my child up for adoption.

"You know, they will want you to stay on for a few years," he responded. That intolerable thought put my bright idea into the Dumpster. All the money and power in the world meant zero to me if the price I had to pay for it was doing more nine-to-five time in a living hell. I felt like I couldn't bear it for another day.

Here I was in the business of restoring order from the chaos in my clients' companies, yet I was unable to take care of my own when it came to the unbearable stress level at my workplace. There was the daily sport of guessing who was going to make the highlight reel of the anger management "play of the day." If someone freaked out in front of a client, which frequently happened, it was a sure winner. There was also the daily onslaught of friendly fire in the form of backstabbing to worry about, which kept me in a never-ending state of hyper vigilance. It came as no surprise that my company was beginning to get a terrible reputation for its revolving door of turnover. I looked over the payroll records of the previous few years and saw that the number of terminated employees equaled two employees for every available position; that is, we had twenty-five employees but had fifty or more during that period who didn't make the cut. I thought, "Oh, my God, this can't go on." I had to find a way to solve this, for saving not only the company but also my sanity.

Fortunately, in this case, I didn't have to dig too deeply to get to the bottom of the problem. I knew that I didn't have the right management team in place to be successful. One of the very worst things for a company owner is to be undermined by his or her own team. The team in question had their own ideas about the corporate structure and personnel management, which clashed one hundred and eighty degrees with my philosophy. I was very hands-on and wanted things to stay that way. "You're the boss; you shouldn't be micromanaging," the team of know-it-alls believed. "Other people should be overseeing the operations"—ones in this case who happened to be their buddies. When this didn't go anywhere, they started trying to get other employees on board for an uprising to convince me to see the light. I was baffled by this behavior, and I couldn't understand why I was not getting the right people for the positions I was filling. They had all of the education and experience required for the job, but it wasn't working out! I was at a point of peak frustration, and I finally realized that I could no longer waste my time fighting with people who didn't agree with my management style and philosophy.

So, I started searching for a way to systematically change my recruiting process and find the secret to hiring people with the right attributes. The first important step was outsourcing my human resources function to eliminate potential conflicts of interest within the company. I researched several local firms and interviewed them to make the best determination. I settled on a firm that had success with an innovative recruiting technique. The human resources consultant told me about a form of testing that was developed primarily for hiring and training salespeople, called TriMetrix. The genius of this technology, I soon learned, was that you could set the benchmarks and attributes of what you wanted in a perfect employee to fit a specific job. The test is not a personality test, but it is designed to examine the person's behavior, attitudes, and values and accurately predict how he or she will perform in that job. What is also ingenious is that it is impossible for test takers to rig their answers to look good and correspond to what they predict the boss would want to hear. Instead, it presents hypothetical situations and requires the test taker to make choices and set priorities. For example, "If there was a car accident, what would be the first thing you would do?"

The test measures the four dimensions of normal behavior: how you respond to problems and challenges, how you influence others to your point of view, how you respond to the pace of the environment, and how you respond to rules and procedures set by others.

A couple of my key employees and I sat down and carefully calibrated the TriMetrix test to fit our needs and then tried it out on a couple of new hires. The results were astounding because it gave us pinpoint accuracy not only to find out whether the prospective employee was suitable for our company but also to place that person in a position and on a team that best matched his or her strengths and capabilities.

I was so impressed with TriMetrix that I went ahead and took the test myself. The nine-page evaluation that came back nailed me to a tee. The report began with the basics about my general behavior and how I would choose to do my job. "Nancy has a good sense of urgency. She wants to be seen not only as a team player but also as a leader of the team." So that right there told me that I was an employer and not an employee for a good reason. It went on. "She tends to trust people and may be taken advantage of because of her high trust level." That did sound familiar. "Nancy is good at solving problems that deal with people. She is good at giving verbal and nonverbal feedback that serves to encourage people to be open to trust her and to see her as receptive and helpful. ... She likes to be involved in the decision-making process." That's why I'm so hands-on. "When she has strong feelings about a particular problem, you should expect to hear these feelings, and they will probably be expressed in an emotional manner." Hmm, that might explain why I'm doing this book.

The next section had bullet points talking about my value to the organization, to help recognize my characteristics and put me on the right team. It listed "people oriented, accomplishes goals through people, sense of urgency, optimistic and enthusiastic, positive sense of humor, ability to handle many activities, and verbalizes her feelings." Then there was a long list of do's and don'ts for communicating with me. Included on the do's were "do provide a warm and friendly environment, put projects in writing and with deadlines, leave time for relating and socializing, and read body language for approval or disapproval," among others. On the don'ts were "don't be dictatorial or dictate to her, leave decisions in the air, use a paternalistic approach, take credit for her ideas, talk down to her, be curt, cold, or tight-lipped." This provides more evidence for why I'd make for a less than desirable employee. The last page listed perceptions—those I have of myself and the way others might see me. My self-perceptions were characterized as "enthusiastic, charming, persuasive, outgoing, inspiring, and optimistic." How others might see me was a decidedly different take. Under moderate pressure, tension, stress, or fatigue, they could see me as "self-promoting, overly optimistic, glib, or unrealistic." And under more extreme pressures, "overly confident, poor listener, talkative, and self-promoter." Ouch. The first thing I thought after reading this was "This test is so weird. How did they get all that from these questions?" Again, it's not something you can try to outsmart.

Just to be extra certain, I had my husband, Rick, take it. At first, I was taken aback because it was clear from comparing our profiles that he and I were complete opposites. For example, I was off the charts on urgency, while he was below par. While he had the highest score on attention to detail, I was a big-picture thinker who was bored with the minutia. But I quickly realized it was all true—and it's probably a great reason why we have made such a good team both in marriage and working together.

Before you start thinking that I must own stock in TriMetrix, let me assure you that if there were something that worked better, I would be talking about that instead. All I can tell you is that employee retention quickly became a problem of the past. Armed with this detailed and highly accurate information, my company was better able to put its employees into a superior position to experience success and fulfillment. From there, I had a good foundation from which to make further refinements to the corporate culture that have had high impact on our collective effectiveness, productivity, and contentment. The external pressures and stress levels of the job may not have changed much over the years, but we have. Now, instead of being known for the employee turnstile that almost swept me out the door, we hear instead, "Can I come work for you?"

CHAPTER 13

The Cure from the Inside Out

"How do you stay so calm?" That is one of the most frequent questions I've received over the years from employees, coworkers, and customers observing me in high-stress situations. They wonder how I manage to keep my cool when they are struggling to cope with smaller levels of stress. When we have been intensely focusing for hours on a particular project without a break, they're ready to collapse when they get home. They can't understand why I have so much energy and I'm so upbeat the next day when they feel so wiped out. After seeing this happen time and again, they've come to realize that this is normal for me.

Everyone thinks my behavior is unusual—but I hadn't thought about it at all. After so many people asked me the same thing, I started to wonder why. I couldn't understand why others had so much trouble keeping up with me and why they thought it was so unusual. But it turns out that I had a secret even I didn't know I had. My secret is very important because it is at the core of my success: my ability to deal with highly stressful situations and my ability to reach for and accomplish bigger goals than others. It has been part of my daily life for decades and is integrated so deeply into my way of being that I didn't think that it was the source of anything out of the ordinary.

This story began in 1971, when I was twelve years old. Earlier that year, doctors examined my father, Gilbert Slomowitz, and diagnosed serious heart damage caused by childhood rheumatic fever. They told him that he was looking at only ten years more to live, at best. A tax law specialist with the Internal Revenue Service by day, my father was also an entrepreneur and a futurist, a man with good ideas both in business and in lifestyle that proved to be ahead of their time. Dealing with this new reality, he began exploring ways to improve his health, such as yoga, organic gardening, and a food-as-medicine diet long before these practices had come into mainstream acceptance.

Late in the summer of that same year, my mother, Adele, saw an article in *The Washington Post* about the health benefits of Transcendental Meditation (TM) and handed it to my father. He knew immediately that it was exactly what he was looking for. He took my older brother, Rich, along to an introductory lecture, and they learned the technique that same weekend. From the start, my father's attitude toward life brightened. What was also clear with the passing of time was that the deterioration of his health had slowed markedly. Without a doubt, TM extended his life beyond what medical science had predicted.

For the first year, I was the lone holdout in the family. My mother saw the dramatic changes in her husband and son and decided to take the TM course herself. (If after reading this chapter, you still have any doubts about the remarkable lifelong benefits of TM, all you need to do is meet my mother, who looks and acts two decades younger than her eighty-some-odd years.) But I was more rebellious and independent to the point that I was regarded as a "problem child." I didn't like school and didn't feel like I fit in anywhere.

Instead of sitting and doing meditation like the rest of the family, I spent my time watching television, especially the reruns of old comedies from the 1960s. My favorite of all was *I Dream of Jeannie*, the show starring Barbara Eden as the beautiful genie in the bottle. My father told me that someday my desires, like those of the genie, would be fulfilled more quickly and easily if I learned to meditate. I put this thought aside, but his words just kept coming back to me. Several months later, I asked him to take me to the TM center to learn the technique.

I learned TM and kept doing it primarily because the rest of my family did it. However, I was a typical teenage girl; I had absolutely no interest in Eastern philosophy or the teachings of the Maharishi or becoming involved with other meditators. I was more interested in attending rock concerts. My walls were covered with posters of my favorite bands, and I spent hours alone in my room with my headphones, listening to my favorite songs over and over. My parents would drag me to various TM lectures and special events because they didn't trust me to be home alone, knowing I would probably get into mischief. No one in my family smoked or drank; however, we had a liquor cabinet for guests. Had they left me alone, I probably would have started smoking cigarettes or gotten into the liquor cabinet. The only redeeming value of the TM events was the opportunity to meet boys. All of this should show you where my mind was at the time. It's hard to say what fate would have befallen me had I not started meditating. However, I continued the twice-daily twenty-minute sessions as I entered young adulthood in the same routine manner as I brushed my teeth. It remained unassumingly so year after year until I finally realized what a gift my father had given to me more than forty years earlier.

At last it dawned on me that meditation might be the reason why I'm different, why I have so much more energy than others, and why I stay calm in the most stressful situations. The turning point was when my brother, Rich, joined my company. He brought far more than his skills and focus. Just prior to this, I was talking to my accountant about walking away from my company and doing something completely different. I had become unhappy with the direction my company had taken. I felt like I had lost control and my employees were working at odds with me. Turnover was very high, my employees were openly challenging me, and I was personally picking up the slack every time someone left. I needed to fill a vacant position and knew that my brother's skills were a perfect match. I also knew that I could trust him and that he would not try to undermine me, as others had before him. I agonized over hiring him because I didn't want to be accused of nepotism, but I hired him anyway—and it was one of the best business decisions I've ever made.

After a few months, I started to notice a change in our work environment. I vaguely remembered something about a "ten percent factor" from a TM lecture many years before. The concept was something like this: when ten percent of a population practices meditation, the environment becomes more cohesive. I hadn't given much thought to it when I heard it, because I have little interest in theories. However, with my brother, my husband, and me meditating, we had reached the ten percent factor, and I couldn't deny what I was seeing with my own eyes. It was at this time that I realized it wasn't just me; all three of us were different in the same way.

However, while I now had company, our other employees continued to react in the same old way, and the contrast became more obvious. I began to think that if more employees meditated, things would get even better. So, after wrestling with the decision over several months, I decided to offer TM as a corporate benefit. However, I wanted to be very careful about how I presented this new benefit. I didn't want people to think that if they didn't participate, they would be somehow marked as outcasts from an inner circle. I had felt this way in other companies—the after-hours parties, golf dates, and other social activities that employees felt they had to participate in to curry favor with the boss in order to get ahead. I also didn't want people to think that I was a weird New Age type—it is so not who I am. I agonized over every word in the memo again and again to make sure it was clear that this was completely voluntary, without strings.

The memo invited everyone to an introductory lecture at our office. I sat quietly in the audience to see how everyone would react. To my surprise, two people signed up immediately for the course. The next year, we held the lecture again, but this time I decided to open up a little bit on a personal level. I stood up and explained in simple terms what TM had done for me. This time, six more signed up, and within a few months, there was a complete culture change in the company. There was a cohesion that had never existed before. Nothing else had really changed in our daily routine, so it became obvious that TM had made the difference.

I was surprised to see that the first people to sign up were the ones I thought were the least likely to do so. One of these people had a combustible combination of quick temper and lack of focus. He decided to try TM because of what he had seen and admired in me. He told me, "You're so consistent. Every day you come in and you say the same thing. I've never seen it anywhere else. And you never hold a grudge. I thought I knew it all when I got here, but I realize I didn't know squat." He said I was the only employer who had taken a real interest in him. "If you give me one little tidbit, one little glimmer, I'm willing to work with you," I had told him. The timing of the TM lecture could not have been better—for both of us.

The change once he started meditating was dramatic, and everyone noticed it. He was able to focus better on his work. He began taking more care. He listened. He became less angry with himself and with others, and the harmony of the whole group around him improved dramatically. With these additional employees practicing TM, our team finally gelled.

The benefits didn't stop there. Those who took advantage of this program began to feel for themselves this invisible shield against stress. Many remarked how they began to see things more clearly and how their energy felt much more positive. Lack of focus is deadly in our work, taking its toll on energy levels, but now people were able to stay in the zone for far longer than before. Others around them began to comment on how much better they looked and other positive changes. The biggest payoff was seeing the anger and negativity within our group dissolve. All this for the price of just closing your eyes twice a day for twenty minutes.

CHAPTER 14

When Not to Quit

When I was eleven years old, my parents took me to a school psychologist by the name of Dr. Sigmund Pickus. That's a promising-sounding first name for a shrink, and I was there to see him for good reason. To say that I was a difficult child would be an understatement. "Why is everything such a problem with you?" my mother complained. "Why can't you be more like your brother?"

"You are going to have problems with her later in life," Dr. Pickus told my parents after they had to pick me up from a week-long school-sponsored camping activity after only two days. What an optimist! Among the leading factors he pointed out was my track record as a serial quitter. Obviously, by removing me from the camp early, my parents were "giving in" to my quitter mentality, and there would be dire consequences for doing so. Of course, my desire to leave had nothing to do with the awful conditions we were placed in—and the fact that I was getting sick from the place.

Yes, it was also true that if I thought something was a waste of time or, worse yet, if things got too unpleasant and hateful for my sensibilities, I was gone. And, yes, it was a source of great frustration to my parents. The most obvious and biggest flashpoint was school. However, the camp experience had nothing to do with that problem, and I really resented his comments at the time. Fortunately, my family agreed with me—that's why they picked me up from the camp after two days—and it became a joke that we would repeat many times over the years when I actually *was* contemplating quitting. "What would Dr. Pickus say about that?" was a catchphrase often recited when the situation really warranted it. My quitter mentality was a problem not only in the early grades of school but also later in my education and career. I left art school after two semesters and didn't finish my business degree until much later in my life, after I had already been in the corporate world for quite some time.

Part of the issue I faced but didn't really fully grasp until much later in life had to do with understanding my learning style. Different people process information in different ways. I came to understand (by accident) that I learn best by observing and repeating information and going at my own pace. This is a concept that has been studied and proven true over the years but did not exist when I was growing up. Without that knowledge and without teachers who are trained to deal with different learning styles, it can be a frustrating experience for all parties involved: parents, teacher, and student.

So while I would quickly grasp practical concepts, I had a terrible time with more abstract things, such as algebra. Also, if the teacher went too fast or presented the material in too rigid a style, I would find it hard to understand and retain the concepts. If the instructor wouldn't work with me to slow it down, I would easily become so frustrated that I wanted to quit. Luckily, with algebra, the teacher quickly recognized that there was a problem and recommended that I get a tutor, which took me from a potential failing grade to an A for the class!

This background is an important prelude to a very difficult challenge I had to face, one that most of us eventually have to deal with in one way or another at our workplaces. When in the middle of it all, you are not going to grow or learn if you are rigid.

Unless your situation is close to paradise, you are going to have to face your share of toxic people. What brings it all to a boiling point is when someone comes forward who seems to have nothing more important to do than to try to make your life a living hell.

In the particular story I am about to share, I want you to know that Dr. Pickus's dire prediction about my life as a quitter had stayed with me since those adolescent days. On many a day when I thought I had reached the end of the end of my rope, I heard his words. I wanted to prove him wrong, and that most certainly gave me that little extra dose of fortitude and grit to persevere.

But things got so bad that I had reached a point where I was ready to admit that Dr. Pickus was right. I went through the motions to leave my company, sell it off, or do anything to avoid having to spend another moment in a situation that was totally intolerable. As I have mentioned before, my line of work can bring out sharp knives in people who view me as a threat to their self-serving fiefdom. But the case of Mandy was completely off the charts.

I knew that it was going to be trouble from the first second I met her. Her predecessor, Joe, was retiring, but he stayed on for a short while during the transition. I happened by to drop off some paperwork to him, and his replacement was sitting there with him in the office. "Oh, Nancy, by the way, this is Mandy. She's going to be your new boss." It was as if I hadn't entered the room. Normally, the ritual of meeting the boss for the first time involves at least the effort of making eye contact, shaking hands, and some conversation along the lines of "looking forward to working with you." But Mandy did not contract a single neck muscle to look in my direction. "OK," I thought to myself. "I get the sense that this is not going to be a happy situation." A few seconds later, I had a more specific thought: "I am going to be in deep trouble here."

"I'd like to meet with you to go over the new direction of your contract," read the e-mail I received from her the very next day. I walked to her office at the appointed hour.

"Here's how it's going to be," she announced. "We're going to get rid of all this stuff in your statement of work that doesn't make sense. We're going to simplify things because we don't want to be bothered by all this stuff you're doing."

At first impression, Mandy seemed like someone who had her act together. She was average in height, weight, and looks, but she knew how to put herself together to make a solid impression. Her bold hair styling accentuated by dangling geometric-shaped earrings and well-tailored attire combined to make a statement of confidence, intelligence, and authority. She had a businesslike and articulate way of expressing herself and without any tinge of emotionality. Although she was several years younger than I, she was also old enough to supposedly know right from wrong.

We hear all the time how overregulated everything is, how the burden of all the red tape stands in our way, needlessly tying our hands and hobbling us unnecessarily in this time of intense global competition. However, there are fundamental business principles that are necessary to defend the integrity of our system, prevent abuse, and avoid disorder and chaos. Eliminating business rules that are designed to protect the system, such as the segregation of accounting from operations, not only is highly inappropriate and bad business but also can become financially devastating.

So, this talk of "we don't want to be bothered by all this stuff you're doing" was the first indication of the yearlong battle I would face as "good vs. evil." Mandy had represented herself to her new boss as an experienced business manager who was going to "show me how things needed to be done." She made it clear from our first meeting that she wanted to reduce the amount of "red tape" being caused by my function, so that the organization could become more "nimble" and get things done faster. Out the window were things like "checks and balances" that stood in the way of purchasing and other decisions that needed to be made. She did not seem to interest herself with the overall business function and the larger processes and systems under our purview that were more critical to the corporation's well-being. Instead, she focused on small areas of activity that she was better equipped to understand, such as invoice processing, which actually ran very smoothly.

What seemed obvious was that Mandy was given a mandate from her supervisors to get rid of me—to do everything and anything to impair my ability to carry out my functions. To that end, she began with a method of slow torture. I don't know whether secret police organizations have used this idea, but if not, then it is only a matter of time before they do. What Mandy did was bombard me relentlessly with e-mails, averaging about twenty or thirty per day. "Why are we doing this?" "There is an infraction, and I need to look at such-and-such invoice." It was important that I answered every one of them. If I didn't, she had another thing to find fault with. I finally confronted her about why it was so important to revamp the invoicing system when it had operated flawlessly. I got specific with her. "We'd have interest penalties if there was a problem, and we haven't had one since I started here." "I'll decide what's important," she barked back via e-mail, which is where the bulk of our interactions played out.

She even questioned the way I signed my e-mails, saying my informality was against company policy; she didn't care that it was how her predecessor had specifically asked me to do this. Quite obviously, this tremendous waste of time was her attempt to build a case against me to prove that I was not performing under my contract. Her mission, as assigned by her new boss, was to tear down the financial operations, and she went about it with unrelenting dedication. When not writing the voluminous e-mails to me, she also worked on turning other colleagues against my group. Come hell or high water, she was going to make her name on fixing "the financial problem."

When it appeared that getting rid of me on the basis of the invoices was not going to work, she took another tact to restructure my contract and to cut back my workload and associated funding. Thankfully, Joe had developed a comprehensive work statement and contract into which it was almost impossible to shoot holes. It didn't make her job any easier that we worked methodically on task to fulfill all our obligations in the contract.

So, while Mandy did not have an easy job ahead of her from a factual perspective, she was a tough adversary because she was smart without letting her emotions get in the way. Being emotional can negate the intellect. But everyone has his or her own weaknesses and flaws—and like trying to beat a great chess master, it took a while to find Mandy's weakness. But I finally discovered it. She may have been smart enough to dig to find things and worked hard at trying to discredit me, but her eventual downfall was due to the fact that she wasn't a business expert and she wasn't "legal" smart. Here is where all of my odd jobs working my way up proved to be an asset. I had temped at a law firm, where I learned the art of documentation—how to organize and sort information right down to the color tab file separators. It took considerable time to pull together the entire paper trail of all the various e-mails from Mandy, but I thoroughly documented the sequence of events. I then took the documentation to a top lawyer to review. It was an expensive move, but it was well worth it. The lawyer prepared a polite but strong letter that went out under my signature and clearly demonstrated that Mandy's actions were in direct violation of our contractual agreement. The letter was fully supported by documentation and would be followed up with serious legal actions if not immediately addressed. It was the beginning of the end for Mandy. The senior managers realized that I was not just going to "take it" and would definitely fight back—in a strong and embarrassing way. The tension and negative behaviors did not go away, but much of the wind was taken out of Mandy's sails. She was no longer viewed as quite so "smart," and others started to see that she was maybe not as business experienced and savvy as she had led them to believe. Soon after, Mandy was no longer in charge. More importantly, other more senior managers began to look at the bigger picture and question her recommended changes.

What made the Mandy situation particularly challenging was the fact that she was a masterful adversary. She was akin to that intimidating player on another sports team you hate to face but would jump at the chance to have on your side. Under different circumstances, Mandy is someone I would have hired. Given the right mandate, she would have been an asset. Looking back, she was given a task that had little chance at a successful outcome. She knew I wasn't going to go along with her game or go down easily. She was probably also embarrassed at some of the things that she had to do.

The most surprising outcome of this entire situation is how I changed. Dealing with such a deadly foe, someone who was given a clear mandate to do everything to destroy me, made my life miserable, again to the point that I seriously wanted to jump ship. Even my strongest employees look back on that experience and tell me that they don't know how I was able to persevere. At the lowest point, I decided that I needed a positive focus to preserve my sanity, something as significantly positive as my work experience was negative. I decided to execute the one item on my "bucket list" for a milestone birthday, which was several months away. One of my favorite rock groups is the Eagles and my favorite musician is Don Felder, the lead guitarist of the Eagles. It had always been my dream to meet Don. I was in awe of his musical creativity and skill, but I was also interested in his story. I read his book *Heaven and Hell, My Life in the Eagles* during this period and drew parallels between our circumstances, admiring his ability to rise above the problems he had with the band.

I thought, why not ask and see if he would play at my event. To my complete surprise, it was not as impossible as it seemed at first, although there were a lot of details to be worked out over the next few months. I invited all my employees to share in this event with me - the evening was even more fabulous than I had imagined. There were many unexpected rewards from doing this, both for myself as an employer and for my employees. This experience taught me several valuable lessons. First, nothing is impossible. Second, don't give up. Third, hold onto your dreams and they will take you far. My employees saw me survive this difficult period and they saw that, through determination, I was able to to fulfill a lifelong dream.

For quite some time, a photo I kept of Mandy, taken from a company picnic, had only one proper place—the dartboard. Yet today, that photo fills me with total gratitude. Thanks to her, I learned so much about myself and what it took to break through to the next level. In fact, I could symbolically dedicate this book to her because the situation gave a whole new depth to my business sensibility and human interaction that I never had before. Mandy challenged me to take a hard look in the mirror, and as a result, I learned a very valuable lesson. How was I treating my employees? I asked myself. Was I guilty of the same insensitivities? How were my attitudes and actions negatively impacting those around me?

The new Nancy reborn out of the fire was a more compassionate and patient person. And were he still alive, Dr. Pickus would be happy to know that I didn't quit.

CHAPTER 15

It's a Two-Way Street

Would I want to go to work for someone like me? That question was foremost in my mind as I contemplated starting my own company. I knew there had to be a better way to run a business than what I had seen throughout my career. This was a major reason for starting my own business—to put my own ideas into action. In the years before I took that step, I had worked for businesses of different sizes and in different industries: finance, retail, legal, fashion. In each of these, I experienced both good and bad. The good ideas I've stored away as something to emulate or adopt. The bad ideas I've stored away as things to avoid or to modify in a positive way before implementing them. In each of these positions, I've made my own mistakes as a worker, colleague, and boss. All of these experiences came together in my mind as I planned how I wanted my business to operate. In this chapter, I'll share with you some of these stories and show you how they impacted my company and continue to do so.

Since we work as consultants to our customers, my employees often sit at a customer site in a physical environment over which I have little or no control. Similarly, I have little or no control over the behavior and decisions of my customers and how they impact my employees. However, what I can control is how I choose to run my company and how I choose to treat my employees. To me, a satisfied customer is a failure. A satisfied employee is a failure. Satisfaction won't keep customers' or employees' loyalty. Instead, I strive to constantly outshine everyone else and demonstrate through our performance how much better we are than the competition. The idea is to create "raving fans" (a term coined by Ken Blanchard and Sheldon Bowles in their book, *Raving Fans)* of both my customers and my employees. How I do this isn't rocket science, and other companies accomplish it just as well as mine does. However, they are rare because this approach runs counter to the prevailing mentality of most businesses as they try to deal with problems during economically challenging times.

It all emanates from a core passion for what I do, along with the fundamental fact that I'm not in this just to make money but to provide a service and to be the best at providing that service. The fact that I understand the work my employees do because I have done each and every job they perform (and I know exactly what each job requires) is not to be underestimated. I am involved in all aspects of my company, and I'm constantly talking to both my employees and my customers. As a result, when there is a problem, I don't have to depend on the opinions of either, and I can act based on facts observed firsthand. This has created loyalty from both ends. My customers have learned that I will always do the right thing: if I'm wrong (or one of my employees is wrong), I will admit it and correct the situation. If the customer is wrong, I will make it clear why and try to figure out how we can work through the issue. This is critical; I offer solutions that don't offend or put others on the defensive, and I reinforce the notion that we are all part of the same team. This approach has failed me only on very few occasions. In many companies, especially where the owner's primary goal is to make money, the boss does not have a real grasp on what the employees actually do. These sorts of bosses aren't able to help coworkers when they experience problems, and they tend to take sides, either sticking up for their employees (which alienates the customer) or siding with the customer (which alienates the employees). By not being "out for myself," it is easier to find solutions when both parties know that I have their best interests at heart.

The seeds for my approach were planted decades ago, when I was very green and just starting out. I was hired as an accountant for a small PR firm. During the interview, they neglected to tell me several important aspects of my job. First, they didn't tell me (and I didn't ask) where I would be sitting. It turned out that my office was—literally—a closet so cold that I had to wear an overcoat just to keep from shivering. The cold air coming from the ceiling vent felt like an arctic wind and turned my "office" into a wind tunnel. Second, they didn't tell me that they were having cash flow problems and that I would be fielding calls from vendors asking (or, more accurately, often screaming) to be paid. The firm had developed many creative ways of avoiding payment, none of which fooled its vendors. Yet everyone in the office adopted this behavior as "normal" and told me that I would just have to "work around it." I didn't last long in that job, and it wasn't the only company I encountered that strategically left out critical job characteristics in the interview. However, I took away some valuable lessons. First, I always show a prospective employee where he or she will sit. Second, I make sure that I explain the job completely, both good and bad. In fact, I often paint a picture that is worse than the actual job. As a result, when the new employees start, they often tell me that the job is better than they expected.

At a prominent law firm where I worked, the partners tried to provide a supportive environment by offering free snacks to their employees. The fridge was always filled with sodas and the cabinets with chips, cookies, and other treats. That was the good side. Unfortunately, the lawyers had such huge egos that the office became a political minefield. I didn't like the politics, but I did like the idea of free snacks. This has become part of my benefits program—but not the unhealthy selections offered by the firm. Instead, we provide a free "healthy snacks" program for all our employees. This program doesn't cost much, but it's very popular.

While the law firm suffered from an overabundance of egos, some of the firms I've worked for went out of their way to minimize the structures that reinforce such behavior. One firm, a former Big Eight accounting firm, didn't assign titles. I was also impressed that each employee, regardless of his or her position in the firm, received business cards and notepads printed with the company logo and his or her name. The partners tried to make everyone feel valuable, a lesson I took with me to my own company to help level the playing field for all. Everyone in my company is an "analyst" regardless of how many years of experience he or she may have or what titles he or she may have had at other firms. Part of this is because of the complexity of what we do; it often takes several years for new employees to fully master their jobs despite lots of prior experience. Some of our more junior employees, because they have worked with me for several years, may provide guidance to new, more experienced employees. It takes some people a while to adjust to this environment, but for those who do, the resulting humility supports the customer service approach for which we are known.

The accounting firm had one benefit I didn't adopt. The management had a ceremony each month to give out "Be Best" awards. This type of award is common to many companies as an attempt to reward the good work of exceptional employees. Maybe the idea is to encourage others to strive for greatness, as the "Be Best" recipients have done. While the intention was well meaning, I think it ultimately backfired. "I worked as hard as the winners!" and "Why is it that the same five people are always the ones who get recognized?" the others often grumbled, mostly to themselves. In my company, at our year-end holiday party, every employee who has completed a year of service receives a special commemoration and gift to honor their loyalty and commitment. Everyone with the same years of service receives the same present, and with each successive year of service, the gift becomes progressively nicer. The range of gifts includes desktop clock and pen sets, digital photo frames, audio electronics, and gift certificates to major stores. The employees look forward to this each year, and, unlike other companies, everybody goes away happy. The price tag is not that expensive, but the payoff is huge.

The annual office party is another of those classic favorites currently listed on the endangered species list, even though the per-employee cost is relatively low. In the frenzy of cutbacks, the company holiday party or summer picnic is an easy target for elimination. However, I think there are fun and creative ways to bring everyone together as a group, even when funds are limited. Few things give me more satisfaction than my annual holiday party. These parties have become legendary but not because they are lavish. They are elegant, from the decorations, to the food, to the sometimes celebrity entertainment, but I think that what really makes our parties special is the fact that I, as the owner of the company, make a personal investment in the event. I want the employees and their spouses/partners to have a special evening—my way of showing them how grateful I am for their contributions to our success. I am involved in all of the planning: the decorations, the food, the entertainment, the years-of-service gifts—even the holiday gift bag that each employee receives. Every year, my family comes together at Thanksgiving, after enjoying a full holiday meal, to create the gift bags for each employee in an assembly-line fashion.

Every employee gets this gift bag, whether he or she has worked with us for one day or ten years. Into these bags go a company calendar, a company pen, a bag filled (by hand) with a variety of chocolates, a card (hand signed), and a gift certificate to a local restaurant. Oh, and there's also a note that their next paycheck will include a generous holiday bonus. I got this idea from a doctor I worked for as a young girl. I remember how thrilled I was at getting a holiday bonus, although I had been there only a few weeks. I once mentioned to an employee—a reserved macho-type not prone to emotional outbursts—that maybe we should stop the candy bags, that maybe the employees didn't really notice them. His response was immediate and emphatic: "No, you can't do that! We all look forward to them—we know that you've created them yourself." True, we are a small company, and this would be difficult if we had several hundred employees. But if we were larger, I would find some other way to express my personal gratitude to my employees for their contribution to our success, something that they would know came from me and wasn't purchased at a store or put together by an underling.

In the current economy, many businesses are being forced to make hard decisions as costs increase and profits decline. Many scale back and even eliminate key benefits such as health insurance and pension plans to reduce costs. Sometimes these companies have no option. All too often, the choice is between scaling back benefits and reducing profits (and the salaries and/or bonuses of the top executives). Predictably, it's the benefits that lose—and the employees who usually suffer.

I believe that developing and maintaining a team of dedicated and loyal employees is the best long-term strategy for a company's success. Organizations with employees who have been with them for ten or twenty years are truly becoming a rare breed. You even see it mentioned in company profiles on Web sites as an accomplishment they're proud of, and it's a refreshing sign of an organization that probably has its head screwed on right.

The way to keep good employees is definitely not by cutting benefits. There is no bigger wet blanket for employee morale than reducing an important benefit or increasing the employee share of a benefit's cost. I know, because I remember how I've felt in such situations. It's not difficult to offer a solid benefit program without breaking the company financially. It's a question of priorities. Some companies provide a smorgasbord of different benefits, many of which are used by only a few employees. However, when the economy goes south and revenues plummet, these programs become a target for the cutting board. Rather than provide a plethora of benefits, I decided to focus on the few quality benefits I feel are critical to my employees' well-being. I can manage these benefits without additional staff, which helps to keep my costs low and enables me to keep the employee share at a minimum. In so doing, I have never had to cut these programs, even as costs for some have skyrocketed.

At the end of the day, there is nothing more valuable to employees and their families than medical and retirement plans. These should be the highest quality a company can afford and should have as little cost impact on the employee as possible. Every year, my outside accountant wastes his breath chiding me about how much I could save by going with a lower-cost health plan. "Nonnegotiable," I tell him. Beyond the employees' peace of mind for having coverage, I think it makes for a healthier (and therefore more productive) workplace. Consider this: if your annual deductible is low and your doctor visit is only a twenty- or thirty-dollar co-payment, you may see a doctor more promptly when health problems arise. It's not just about someone coming to work sick and spreading a cold or flu to others. Think about the life-saving possibilities of detecting cancer, diabetes, or cardiovascular disease in the early stages. Instead, because of high deductibles and co-pays, many employees put off procedures until the consequences are far more severe and their options compromised.

The retirement plan has a similar level of importance, even if your employees don't realize it. Most companies will match employees' contributions to their 401(k) plans, up to a limit, often quite small. Many employees live in the present and don't voluntarily contribute to their 401(k) plans, especially younger employees. As a result, there is no match—and no investment. We don't match funds based on employees' contributions to their 401(k)s; we contribute to this plan through our profit-sharing program. In doing this, I ensure that each employee will have at least something toward retirement, regardless of whether he or she voluntarily contributes.

This notion of "becoming the company I would want to work for" is a simple quest but one with more profound consequences than most of us might consider. To those organizations that will scoff at what I have just presented, I say to them, "Check out my results." The concept of having both a profitable company and a happy cadre of coworkers doesn't have to be an oxymoron in today's harsh world. Instead, it is a formula for success and sustainable growth that needs to go back on the front burner.

CHAPTER 16

Check Your Ego at the Door

Check your ego at the door—I believe that this should apply to everyone in the workplace. I exemplify this behavior in my own company and insist that my employees follow suit. While it's not easy to get people to do this, I set a strong example and expect this of my employees regardless of their qualifications and experience levels.

Most people think that running a company is a glamorous job. They are shocked to learn that I work harder than any of my employees, that I rarely take time off, and that preserving my company's reputation is my number one priority. I don't sit in an ivory tower and count my money. I care deeply about the quality of the services delivered by my company and the welfare of my employees. I treat everyone with dignity and respect regardless of his or her position within the company. Unfortunately, this appears to be a rare situation in today's business world.

Many of the business owners I've come across over the years have focused exclusively on the fruits of the company and the trappings of success. Vanity items, such as fancy offices, shiny company cars, and expensive furniture, are pursued rather than building a solid infrastructure of the organization. Overhead can be good, and it can be bad. Focusing too much on the vanity items can be a recipe for disaster in building a solid and long-term company.

A true leader has a servant mentality. Here is the philosophical difference between me and other business owners on how best to operate a business. They can't understand why I take such an active role with the employees and customers and in overseeing the services we deliver, and they wonder why I don't just let others run the company for me. They don't understand why I don't have a fancy corporate office with a large mahogany desk, a company car, and five assistants walking around behind me. These items are what I call "vanity overhead." I prefer to spend my money on infrastructure and employee welfare.

They can't understand why I don't want to grow into a big company with hundreds more employees when the opportunities to do so are ever present. Don't I want to expand, cash out, retire to the Cayman Islands, and live high on the hog like everybody else? And why am I spending all this money on my employees instead of building my own portfolio? "We just don't get it," they say, shaking their heads.

I've had this attitude throughout my entire career, from my first entry-level position on. I've always done my best regardless of my position or stature in the company and without expectation of anything in return. As such, I've earned the respect of my managers and coworkers. Unfortunately, I haven't seen many others adopting this strategy. It's harder to get ahead this way, and it takes longer to get there, but in the long run, it's the right thing to do. Having a good work ethic and a small ego may not be the norm. If you make quality the goal, rather than focusing on short-term gains, success will follow.

In today's world of me-me-me and "I want it all now" (without paying my dues), it's hard to find people of like mind to work for me. I try to groom people this way, leading by example. I make it clear in the interview that this is not a glamorous job. I tell the new prospective employee, "Yours is an important and high-profile job, but you will be in the trenches. Do you like to solve puzzles? Can you work in the weeds?" I sometimes dump a pile of spreadsheets on the table during the interview and ask, "How would you handle this task? How would you go about analyzing this information?" If the candidate doesn't run screaming from the room, he or she has a fighting chance of making it here. Once hired, I put the new hire through my own form of boot camp: making copies and other seemingly menial tasks are all part of the initiation process.

Another technique I apply as early as the first interview is to paint the picture about five hundred times worse than the job is going to be. If that doesn't scare them off, that's a good start. Once in the trenches, they usually come to the realization that this is not as bad as they thought it was going to be—much better than the opposite experience of a rosy expectation turned sour.

At the end of the day, it all goes full circle back to the servant example I try to set as their boss. Whether I'm there at the Xerox machine or filling in for someone who is sick, they see that I am not too good for this work and I am not aloof on some high pedestal. This servant thing is also a spirit that can be contagious. It is delightful when others step up without being asked if someone needs help or is having difficulty.

A number of years ago, I read an essay, written by American business educator Robert K. Greenleaf, that validated my ideas about leadership. The essay, "The Servant as Leader," was inspired by a story about a group of pilgrims in Herman Hesse's *Journey to the East* and illustrates the true characteristics of a leader. In the story, everything had been going exceptionally well for the travelers until the departure of their servant, Leo. When he left, the entire pilgrimage degenerated into disharmony and came to a premature end. One of the pilgrims went in search of Leo to find out why his departure had this effect on the group. After a lengthy and arduous search, he found the servant; Leo was the spiritual leader of a large monastery. Leo had been leading the pilgrims quietly through his words and actions. He didn't need a fancy title and was content to perform his menial duties without complaint. Using Leo as an example, Greenleaf defined the abilities an enlightened leader should have: listening, empathy, awareness, foresight, stewardship, and a commitment to the growth of people, among many more.

This essay shatters the stereotype of what it truly means to be a leader. Leo had no ego to protect when he was preparing meals and no artificial status to uphold while tidying the tents. The story shows that being a leader is not dependent on having a corner office or scores of employees under your command. Leo's humble nature serves as a poignant reminder that our words and actions are what guide others most effectively. The example we set creates our status as the leader, not the fancy title or the corner office.

CHAPTER 17

Going Retro

We can't turn back the clock, but wouldn't it be nice to get back to some of the old-world manners that seem to be going the way of the dinosaurs? There was a time when relationships mattered, when customer service mattered, when quality mattered. When I think of this kind of relationship-first orientation to business, I think of Ferrell's, a shop in the community where I grew up. It was a beautiful gift store full of unusual, elegant items that you'd never find at Wal-Mart—or even Neiman Marcus. Mrs. Ferrell appreciated everyone who came into her shop. She seemed to remember everyone's name and personal details, down to the fact of knowing how my husband loved chocolate, which she would always offer to him. "Oh, I have some charming things for you," she said in her elegant way. Her care was also evident in how the items were displayed and personally gift wrapped by her: she hand-tied special bows on each package. Her attitude was "I want it to be beautiful for you, so I'm going to take the extra time to make it right." She would talk as she worked, discussing her customers' issues of the day. It was always a comfortable place to shop and not because of the store but because of Mrs. Ferrell herself.

However, Mrs. Ferrell's story is an unfortunate example of what is happening in the business world today. Her new landlord raised the rents for all the stores in her small village mall and unfortunately, Mrs. Ferrell could not afford to pay the increased rent. As a result, the grace and beauty of Ferrell's Gift Shop are now just a memory.

Perhaps why I loved Ferrell's was that it reflected the same spirit of my grandparents' candy store in New Jersey. Over a century ago, they immigrated to America with high hopes and a strong belief that the sky was the limit as long as they worked hard, exercised sound business judgment, provided good value, and cared about their product and their customers. While they were never rich, they were successful and were able to keep their business going through the worst of times, the Great Depression. They did this with hard work and value that were recognized by their customers. For example, they created a new product out of the leftover broken candy that might have been thrown away by another store. On Fridays, they sold a popular one-penny "prize bag" consisting of a potpourri of broken candy pieces. It was a clever idea of dealing with "seconds" that became their hallmark and drove the success of their business. It is something people of that community old enough to still remember recall with great affection to this day.

Mrs. Ferrell's and my grandparents' stores were part of the heartbeat that made our communities strong—before the global economy made them antiquated artifacts. So many similar businesses—family-owned pharmacies, hardware stores, gas stations—have been replaced by large corporate businesses. Something happened when those shops closed. That dedication to providing good service and to fostering great relationships with the people around them closed along with them. It seems that the pride of ownership and professional work ethic that often accompanied these shops also left with them.

Even the large stores have changed. I can remember that the department stores of my childhood carried distinctive product lines. Each store had its own favorite brands, and you could wander among them and discover new things at each place. They've all been bought up by conglomerates now. The stores are beautiful and modern—but they all look the same and all sell the same products. Consistency is much more cost-effective and promotes a positive bottom line. However, what's been lost is individuality and differentiation. Now I search for the few remaining small boutique stores, where the owners do their own buying and cater to their own tastes and their own pride of ownership. You can still find them, but they are fewer in number.

These stores, like everything else in life, are impermanent. As much as I loved going to Ferrell's, I, too, like millions of others, have a busy life with little free time. I love the hassle-free convenience of ordering something online and having it delivered to my doorstep the next day. And the ability to read consumer reviews on a service such as Amazon or eBay injects a small touch of the sensibility that is missing. However, nothing can replace direct human contact and seeing products up close. Those seem to be becoming things of the past.

It's incumbent on business owners to take a step back to reexamine and understand that they have to adapt to the times and sometimes stretch outside of their comfort zones. I have been going to a wonderful country French restaurant for years, Normandie Farm Restaurant, one of those places where everyone on staff has been there forever and all, from the busboy to the head waiter, know your name. It is very genteel, with courtly waiters and white tablecloths, but I started to notice that their clientele was all quite old. "Why aren't they attracting younger people?" I thought to myself.

So, I decided to hold one of my annual holiday parties at the restaurant, thinking that my younger employees could discover how wonderful the place was. I met with the manager and shared with him a vision for an event that included replacing his tables, chairs, tablecloths, and other fixtures. He was willing to embrace change and was surprisingly accommodating. On the day of the event, the restaurant was literally transformed—still a warm country restaurant but with modern stage lighting and dazzling table decorations that enhanced that feeling. The owner of the restaurant was excited and was running around taking pictures of all the changes. Everyone who worked there saw a different way of doing things, without taking away what made it so appealing. And my younger employees all said, "This is cool—we'd like to come back here."

Don't think that I can't see the advantages of many of the technical and business advances we've made over the years. For example, I love living in an old nineteenth-century home, but I'm also glad to have air-conditioning, lights, and indoor plumbing. It's great to send an e-mail, but it's still nice to get a card in the mail or, better yet, a phone call. E-mail and "emoticons" can't convey the feelings that you get with a phone call. Skype is a wonderful tool because you get to see the person you're talking to—even better than a phone call. I can communicate with friends in far-off places in ways I never could before. But many people use it within the same office, as an alternative to walking over to someone's desk and talking in person. It this efficiency, or is it laziness?

Cell phones and PDAs are fantastic devices that have brought us great convenience. However, when I see people walking around with their faces buried in their PDAs or hear stories of young people texting each other while riding in the same car or when I see coworkers sitting through an entire meeting while playing on their BlackBerrys instead of attending to the matters at hand, I think that convenience has been twisted into impersonality The big downside of push-button technology is that it has made the world a colder, tougher place. I don't want to go back to the horse and buggy, but many of the core values of integrity, compassion, and sustainability that worked back then still apply. They should have never been abandoned to the degree we see so evident around us today.

I gravitate toward the ways of the Old World. I realize that my taste in things many may consider antique or antiquated. For example, I love the Vermont County Store, where they still sell Black Jack chewing gum and many of the familiar brands from my childhood that are so hard to find today. When I go into old buildings, I take time to admire the carved stone and wood, relics from a bygone time of craftsmanship that doesn't exist in the modern world. This is why, instead of an expensive modern home, I prefer my one-hundred-eighty-year-old home. At the same time, my mentality is neither romantic nor anti-progress nor fixated only on keeping the status quo.

In fact, I am always embracing change in the form of constantly thinking about how I can improve something. What I try to do is introduce improvements that don't sacrifice the core values that sustain relationships and the commonsense practices that sustain good business decisions. What I've tried to do in this book is show, using examples from my own experience, the types of dysfunctional behaviors that drive us away from those core values and threaten to destroy what those who came before us worked for and fought so hard to create. I've also tried to point out with each example not only what has gone wrong but also what we can do today to rise above that dysfunctional behavior to eliminate the madness in the workplace.

Understand that you won't find me waxing nostalgic about the old ways when it comes down to the labor- and tedium-saving technologies and innovations that make me better able to serve my clients. There is nothing more gratifying than to be able to produce high-quality results instantaneously with the push of a button on something that might have taken me weeks a decade or so ago. But cranking out work at higher speed and productivity has come with a price on our humanity. Every new innovation ups the ante of expectation and stress. Charlie Chaplin, in his 1936 film *Modern Times*, summed it up best—and hilariously— with his out-of-control mechanical contraption to feed factory workers so they wouldn't have to take a break to eat.

I've made one important observation about many of the people who clearly don't feel the same way I do. They criticize the fact that I don't focus on growing my business as they do. They brag about how many new positions they've created while I increase by a few each year—a healthy 20% growth but nowhere like the 100% or more that they are experiencing each year. They question why I work so hard and why I rarely take vacations. I tell them until I'm blue in the face that I want to build something that is strong and lasting. I'm not interested in growing my business overnight so I can make the quick profit. I explain how I want relationships with my employees and clients that are measured in decades and not months, that my growth will be measured by stability and quality and not by profit margins. But they just don't get it. They don't get me. With all their passion and excitement about growth and profit, what I've noticed is that there's something missing in their eyes—a deeper sense of real happiness and contentment. Instant gratification goes only so far.

Many of the issues I've raised in this book are a function of how cold, uncaring, and outright inhospitable our workplaces have become. Customer service seems just as artificial and mechanical and in danger of becoming a thing of the past. Some businesses are making an attempt to be more personal, such as a bank hotline I recently had to call on two successive days. It was obvious that both representatives had it scripted on their screen at about the same time in the conversation to ask me how my day was going.

No matter what we do, the idea of providing good service and fostering great relationships with the people around us should never have to be considered "retro." If each of us made these values a higher priority in our workplaces, think what a measurably better world it would be.

Epilogue

My inspiration and motivation for writing this book deepened over the months I spent writing it—and for good reason. Many of the negative realities in our workplaces we have discussed seem to have gone from bad to worse.

Some people who had read portions of the book in progress chimed in on how strongly the issues I've raised hit home in their daily lives at work, no matter their particular industry or profession. Sadly, far too many of us wake up each morning with a real sense of indignation and dread facing the new day. We feel as though our hopes, dreams, and aspirations of creating a fruitful life for ourselves and our families have been cut adrift. Staying afloat has replaced getting ahead. We question what happened to the moral compass that had guided us.

Those of us who are still fortunate to have jobs often feel trapped in a malaise. "What's the use?" we ask ourselves in futility. If we happen to do our jobs conscientiously, we become frustrated at the incompetence of those around us. Out of ten people in a group, perhaps eight of them don't care about anything more than collecting their paychecks. The ones who do care have to pick up the slack and are forced to do the others' work for them.

The stories I've shared and the issues they highlight were structured to look at what goes on in our workplaces from several points of view, from that of the CEO to those of the workers in the trenches. What I hope you will carry away from this is a broader perspective and a more holistic understanding of the cause and effect our choices and actions can create.

If there are two or three aspects in this book that you can apply to your situation, you may become quite surprised at the profound difference they can make in the quality of your life. Sometimes, even the smallest changes can set off a positive chain reaction. But moving from being a passive participant or victim to being a change agent begins with taking a hard look at yourself in the mirror. It is a process all of us who want to create a better world have to repeat on a daily basis.

I also hope a community will emerge from this that will support its members in the process and inspire others to join. For that reason, I encourage you to share your experiences with all of us at http://www.CompanyRehab.net.

Acknowledgments

To Joel Brokaw for believing in me and for bringing my stories to life. To my husband, Rick, who has the patience of a saint and is the anchor who always brings it home for the team. To my mother, Adele; my brother, Rich; and Uncle Alvin for their unwavering support throughout the years. To my cousin Susan who totally "gets it." And to my friends Robin and Linda, who are always there to listen and provide critical feedback.

References

TriMetrix
The Brooks Group
Sales Assessment Test for Hiring, Training & Coaching
The TriMetrix® Assessment: The Missing Piece in the
    Hiring Puzzle
http://www.brooksgroup.com/assessments

Don Felder
Heaven and Hell: My Life in the Eagles (1974–2001)
Copyright 2008 by Don Felder
John Wiley & Sons, Inc.
Hoboken, New Jersey

Transcendental Meditation
The Transcendental Meditation® (TM) Program
www.tm.org

Vermont Country Store
http://www.vermontcountrystore.com/store/

Raving Fans
Raving Fans, A Revolutionary Approach to Customer Service
Ken Blanchard and Sheldon Bowles
Copyright 1993 by Blanchard Family Partnership and Ode to
    Joy Limited
William Morrow and Company, Inc.
New York